INTRODUCING A NEW HYMNAL

How to Improve Congregational Singing

JAMES RAWLINGS SYDNOR

G3283
G.I.A. PUBLICATIONS, INC.
7404 South Mason Avenue
Chicago, IL 60638

Introducing A New Hymnal — James Rawlings Sydnor

Copyright © 1989, GIA Publications, Inc.
7404 S. Mason Ave., Chicago, IL 60638
International Copyright Secured
All Rights Reserved
Printed in USA

Illustrations by Paul Daeger
Copyright © 1965, World Library Publications

ISBN 0-941050-19-X

PREFACE

This book was written because of messages from two friends. The first came from a pastor having difficulty in introducing a new hymnal. The second came from the Executive Director of the Hymn Society of America who had good reason to be deeply concerned about poor congregational singing he had observed across the country.

The pastor of a large city congregation in the Carolinas telephoned me to say that his people were rebelling because he had been giving them too many unfamiliar hymns from the new denominational hymnal. They had almost quit singing! Could I come down for a week and help "prime the pump?" I accepted his invitation and had a fascinating time with his congregation. We worked on how to approach and learn new hymns and also how to sing old favorites more intelligently. Although the people's hymn singing attitudes and habits were not completely altered by my efforts, they at least had begun a turnabout.

W. Thomas Smith, Executive Director of The Hymn Society of America, had within the past year attended public worship in about thirty congregations of eight denominations across the country. He wrote, "I must frankly state that hymn singing on our continent is in terrible condition. I have not heard vigorous congregational singing during these very active months of travel. This problem is not associated with just a few congregations but is widespread through all regions of North America."

And yet his indictment comes at a time when there is scarcely a denomination which has not within the past decade or so issued a hymnal and many churches are now at work on a new hymnbook. What an anomaly! Many new hymnals — poor hymn singing. How do you explain it? Over fifty years ago Sir Walford Davies, former Master of the King's Music, noting this same phenomenon, wrote, "The first impression one gets as a result of much experience in churches of various types, is that the admirable enterprise shown by the compilers of recent hymnals is not imitated by the users."* Why does this happen? This book will explain some of the reasons.

These two problems — introducing a new hymnal and improving congregational singing — are closely intertwined. I agree that congregational use of hymns is in sad repair in many localities and needs a remedy. If a new hymnal is being introduced, it should be a glorious opportunity not only to inaugurate the new hymnal but also to launch a carefully crafted long-range program of education and training which will lead to great congregational singing.

---

* *Music and Worship*. Walford Davies and Harvey Grace. p. 194. New York: The H. W. Gray Company, 1935. Reprinted by AMS Press, New York, NY.

This manual is designed to give guidance to the leadership of a local congregation in accomplishing these two tasks. I am aware that many readers of this guide may have sparse knowledge of music, so I have attempted to use nontechnical explanations. Experienced musicians, however, will receive helpful information. Also I have kept in mind that these readers are from various denominations. However the hymn singing problems facing these various congregations are remarkably similar.

This book is divided into two sections. The first is devoted to the introduction of a new hymnal and the second section explains how to improve the many factors which influence congregational singing. Either part can be studied first.

Guidance will be provided for the transfer of the treasures of the hymnal to the hearts and lips and lives of every Christian. Its aim is to enable as many members as possible to reproduce in their lives the same measure of devotion and spiritual insight enjoyed by the writers of our hymns. This re-enactment may occur in the private or public reading or singing of hymns. Every sincere motion in this direction will be aided by the gracious assistance of the Holy Spirit.

The rewards of successful introduction of your new hymnal and an increase of vital singing are enormous. Your congregation will be freed to respond with joy to the invitation of God to sing praise in new songs. Visitors to your congregation will feel the genuineness and warmth as your folk express their faith. They may be moved to join your church. Your people will be storing in their memories the testimony to God's purposes and love as expressed by the hymn writers and composers. And as they sing hymns with confidence, they will find themselves drawn closer to their neighbors in the pews. The hymnal, after all, is the song book of Christians who have a right to expect wise guidance in its full use.

The materials for stimulating a magnificent outburst of singing among Christians across this broad land have never been as plentiful as now or of such high caliber. These new hymnals have hundreds of great hymns, many of them brand new. However it is not sufficient just to provide a denomination with an excellent hymnal. A skilled pedagogy is also needed. Issuing a new hymnal without a guide would be like presenting a computer to a customer with no manual to show how to use it.

I wish to express special thanks to YuLee Larner and Austin Lovelace who gave helpful advice in the preparation of this manual.

You are about to embark on a process which can enrich the life of your congregation.

James Rawlings Sydnor
Richmond, Virginia
December, 1988

INTRODUCING A NEW HYMNAL

How to Improve Congregational Singing

TABLE OF CONTENTS

Preface

Part One

INTRODUCING A NEW HYMNAL

Chapter 1
HYMNAL INTRODUCTION:
PLANNING A WORKABLE PROCESS

"I hate the idea of our getting a new hymnal." "Our people are afraid of the prospect of another hymnal." "Why do we need a new hymnbook? Haven't we got enough hymns in our old book?" These are actual statements and questions I have heard from congregational members who know that their denomination is in process of preparing a new book. This anxiety is especially voiced when they learn that their own congregation will be buying this book. On the other hand, of course, there are folk who anticipate a new hymnal with considerable pleasure.

Why are there such strong emotions about new hymnals? A basic reason is that hymn singing is one of the most important parts of public worship for the people. Therefore if this part is made unfamiliar and perhaps difficult to master, an apprehension may be engendered. In the past few years the newspapers have carried stories about the inner workings of hymnal committees which report that some of the members' most beloved hymns are being eliminated. Even if this story originates in another denomination, it frightens many churchgoers. "Will this happen to our book?" Not only do they hear that familiar hymns are to be eliminated but also they learn that the texts are being altered, tune harmonies are changed, and new tunes are being coupled with well known texts. Also they read that within the past generation there has been an explosion of new hymn texts and tunes and the committees want to include a generous number of these. This might mean that some of the old favorites may be squeezed out.

Furthermore we all know that in many churches there is an innate resistance to any change. I am reminded of the story of the aged Scottish beadle whose son was to succeed him. The beadle in Scotland is a minor church official. This old man was on his deathbed. His son leaned over and whispered, "Father, is there any final word you have for me?" The old man rasped out these words. "Resist all improvements."

In spite of these facts, congregations can be prepared to welcome their new hymnal as a "friendly" book which contains many of their favorites. However, it would be wise for them to know from the beginning that not every favorite of every member is apt to be included. They can look forward, though, to many marvelous new hymns which in time will also become their favorites. They can be reminded that not too long ago a hymn tune like CWM RHONDDA (the sturdy Welsh tune for "Guide me, O thou great Jehovah" and "God of grace and God of glory") was brand new in many denominations but now has become a widely known hymn melody.

Here are some of the important aspects of the process.

1. Determining who will manage the hymnal introduction
2. Outlining the goals of this process
3. Surveying the congregation.
4. Reviewing the new hymnal.
5. Understanding the factors which affect congregational singing.
6. Preparing the people to welcome the new book.
7. Using denominational resources
8. Assigning tasks

1. DETERMINING WHO WILL MANAGE THE HYMNAL INTRODUCTION

Any person in a congregation with a concern for great congregational singing can set a brush fire of enthusiasm for the new hymnbook which in time can help transform the people's music. But if this interest is to be translated into tangible results, it can best be begun by selecting a small team or committee from the leadership of the church which can initiate the process.

Its personnel, of course, should include the clergy and the staff musician(s). But it would be helpful to add some members from the Music and Christian Education Committees plus several persons at large. These people do not all have to be musicians. Also this committee could be an introductory exploring committee which, at the conclusion of this first meeting, would assign tasks. However, after a reasonable time, this group might reconvene to assess the progress of the introduction procedures.

Even if the new hymnal has been ordered but not yet received, the committee could profitably meet and begin making plans for its arrival. And, obviously, if you have a recently acquired hymnal, you can set in motion a process for enlarging your use of it.

This group at its first meeting can initiate the introduction process by considering the broad range of topics listed above and perhaps adding others which apply to the needs of your particular congregation. Obviously it will be helpful if committee members will have read this guide before the initial meeting.

2. OUTLINING THE GOALS OF THIS PROCESS

The committee can be encouraged by the fact that the greatest single musical contribution which church leaders can make to their individual congregations is the diffusion of hymns into the total life of the church, especially the development of superior congregational singing when the entire church family assembles for the worship of God.

The first and specific goal is a successful transition from the present to the new hymnal and a gradual welcome introduction of its treasures and resources. A second and more comprehensive objective is the widest possible use of hymns. Here is an outline of some steps leading to a singing church:

- The people need to be trained to read and pray hymns in their private devotional life.
- They can also be encouraged to sing hymns at home with their families and friends.
- Hymns should be incorporated in the educational program of the church.
- The people need regular opportunities for hymn practices.
- The congregation should be given occasions to celebrate their faith in hymn festivals and in informal hymn sings.
- Finally the intelligent and spirited use of hymns in public worship should be a high priority.

We mentioned the importance of the development of great congregational singing. How would you define this goal? Is it having your people sing hymns as loudly as possible?

Here is one definition. Great congregational singing is being achieved when the entire congregation sings a sizable number of good hymns with spiritual perception and musical artistry.

It is quite possible that many congregations whose leaders are reading this manual already have good congregational singing. There is always room for improvement. If, however, the hymn singing of your people leaves much to be desired, it will help if at least some of the committee members have heard exhilarating congregational singing at some other church, a hymn festival, church music conference, seminary convocation, annual meeting of the Hymn Society of America or on a recording. These experiences will serve as models of great congregational singing.

3. SURVEYING THE CONGREGATION

In any educational process it is essential to know where the learners are in knowledge and skill. Then a plan of instruction can be based on this understanding. Success is much more assured.

In making a determination of the state of singing in your church, there are at least three approaches to this congregational survey. First, the committee members can discuss their own general perceptions of the congregation's tradition of hymn singing, the strength of their nostalgia for the old hymns, their singing abilities, and their attitudes toward change in general. Second, a study and tabulation can be made of the hymns and briefer liturgical musical items which have been sung in public worship over the past ten years. This will inform the committee of the present repertoire of congregational song. See page 10 of this chapter for a bulletin board way of informing the people of their hymn experience for the past several years. Third, a skillfully designed questionnaire can determine the congregation's knowledge and attitudes regarding their singing.

Leaders who have used this third method testify that the information gained has been very helpful in planning a program of hymn instruction. In these days of large scale migration from one denomination to another, we find diversity of hymn background and desires in almost every congregation.

After stating the purpose of this questionnaire, here are some of the questions from which you could select items for your survey:

HYMN QUESTIONNAIRE
- ---   In what denomination were you raised?
- ---   Can you read music? No___ Some___ Yes___ (Check one)
- ---   Do you know any hymns from memory? How many?

  _____
- ---   Do you have a hymnbook in your home?
- ---   Do you use hymns in your private devotions?
- ---   Would you like to have some occasions when you and others could sing hymns requested by you and the others?
- ---   Age bracket? Under 25___ 25-50___ Over 50___
- ---   Any suggestions for improving our congregational singing?

--- Please list your ten favorite hymns.

Name _____

If deemed wise, the questionnaire could add a note saying signature is not required. This questionnaire could be sent to every person in your congregation by means of the parish newsletter or could be inserted in the Sunday morning bulletin. Include a cutoff date for returning them to the church office. Using a more limited procedure, you could give two of these questionnaires to each member of the adult choir and ask these singers to fill out one form and give the other for completion to a member of the congregation. Each chorister is responsible for returning both forms by a certain date. Some committee member could collate these returns and make a report of findings to the entire committee.

4. REVIEWING THE NEW HYMNAL

When the new hymnal is available, one member should be prepared to "walk" the group through the hymnbook touching the high spots. This person could summarize the preface, explain the table of contents which defines the topical structure and distribution of the hymns, describe the indexes and their purposes, explain the general nature of the hymns and the liturgical material. Save time for singing at least a few of the newer hymns. This reviewer will find information about hymnal design and contents in Chapter 2. A more thorough study of the new book and further singing of hymns, if desirable, could be done at a later meeting.

Underlying the pragmatic introduction of a new hymnal is recognition of the fact that in many new hymnals perhaps one third to one half of the hymns will be new and probably unfamiliar to most of your people. Since many denominational hymnals have from four to seven hundred hymns, this means that the committee will find several hundred new hymns. How in the world can all or even a majority of these hymns be blended into the public worship of a single congregation and into the individual lives of its members?

When I am faced with enormous problems and opportunities like these, I recall that a minister friend of mine and his sexton one morning stepped onto the front porch of his church after a particularly heavy windstorm had strewn the big lawn with branches and twigs. The minister said, "Bob, how are you going to cope with all this mess?" Bob answered, "I just pick up one stick at a time." So the introduction of new hymns can be successfully accomplished by dealing with them one by one.

An early task would be to make a list of hymns (noting especially the tunes) which are already familiar to most of the members — hymns like "Holy, Holy, Holy, Lord God Almighty" and "The Church's One Foundation." Publish this list in the parish newsletter to reassure the congregation that the new book will be a "friendly hymnal." Urge the people not to prejudge the hymnal.

W. Thomas Smith, Executive Director of The Hymn Society of America, suggested that, when the list of hymns to be included in a new hymnal is published, the clergy and musicians should use only those hymns on this list which are known by the congregation until the new book appears. And the leaders should inform the people that, in effect, they are already using the new book. The worshipers will know then that many of their favorites will be included. This will help to make it a companionable book when it arrives.

After this list of familiar hymns is made, the group or a subcommittee should then compile a list of new hymns to be introduced during the first year. Arrange these in various categories (for example; praise, season, communion, dedication). It would also be helpful to think ahead and develop a tentative five-year projection.

5. UNDERSTANDING THE FACTORS WHICH AFFECT CONGREGATIONAL SINGING

Any planners considering the improvement of congregational singing need to know that there are many factors which, for good or bad, affect the quality and quantity of the singing. It is a rare and fortunate parish in which all these factors are positive. Great congregational singing does not happen accidentally. Each of the following items will affect the singing to a greater or lesser extent. Discussion of most of these factors constitutes the second part of this book.

• *Music literacy.* Recognize that many of your people cannot read music. If your congregation were the student body of a choir college or the attendees of a church music conference, you could announce any hymn in the book and hear the congregation sing with great confidence and beauty. Because these musicians can read music notation with ease, this means that they do not have to worry about the notes but can concentrate on the text. But such a congregation is a rarity. Therefore your hymnic tuition must be adapted to the fact that many people learn their hymns by rote. We will have much more to say about this procedure in later chapters, especially Chapters 3 and 6.

• *Hymn singing tradition.* The spiritual vitality, singing habits, hymnals, and leadership of former generations in a congregation will manifest themselves in the present singing. Consequently it is smart to understand the hymnic content and methods used by predecessors in your church.

- *Clerical leadership.* The spiritual leader (whether priest, minister, or rabbi) has a crucial role in the development of strong congregational singing. By intelligent choice of hymns, by assisting in the development of a long-range program of hymnic education, and by contagious example of singing during public worship, the clergy can be a powerful force in cultivating the spirit of song in their congregation. See Chapter 4.

- *Music leadership.* The principal responsibility for the development of congregational music is ordinarily lodged in the staff musician. She/he will exercise it in the planning of educational strategy and in the skill of playing hymns and teaching them to the congregation and the choirs. And, if there is a cantor (song leader), this person by gesture and verbal tuition can encourage the singers and help them to express the ideas and emotions of the hymns. Of special importance is the tonal design and location of the pipe organ. This has a marked effect on hymn singing. See Chapter 5 for information about organ design and selection.

- *Acoustics.* In sanctuaries with good acoustics, the members of the congregation will feel uplifted when singing. They can hear one another easily, and consequently they will feel more like a community of believers. See Chapter 9.

- *Choirs.* The primary function of choirs is to join with all other members of the congregation in offering worship to Almighty God and, in so doing, to lead the congregation in worship through hymns, anthems, and in the sung portions of the liturgy. See Chapter 5.

- *Training and singing opportunities.* The presence or absence of many opportunities for singing hymns (in addition to public worship) and the custom of hymn practices affect congregational singing. Sir Walford Davies wrote, "There ought to be a regular system of adding to the repertory. Where congregational practices are held, a new hymn — even two — should be learned on every occasion; and the hymns so learned should be used fairly frequently during the ensuing month or two, in order that they may become established."* See Chapters 6 and 10.

The committee needs to discuss these and other factors and compare them with the local situation. Some can be changed soon, others must be put on the back burner. In this determination, the members can keep in mind Reinhold Niebuhr's famous prayer: "God, grant me the serenity to accept the things I cannot change, the courage to change the things I can, and the wisdom to know the difference."

---

* *Music and Worship,* p. 194.

6. PREPARING THE PEOPLE TO WELCOME THE NEW BOOK

It is never too early to begin preparing a congregation for a new hymnal. Even if the publication date is far down the pike, begin the process of preparation. An Episcopal clergyman said, "the biggest problem in teaching a new hymnal to congregations is trying to teach too much too soon without adequate preparation." Then he says. "Adequate preparation includes at least two ingredients: letting the congregation know that many familiar elements are still intact, and providing sufficient rehearsal time."

Unfortunately there are many parishes where the only concern for congregational singing seems to be the selection of three hymns whose numbers are printed in the bulletin. But as you begin to do some of the following things, the congregation will understand that the leadership is concerned about the people's part in public worship and is committed to preparing them for the new book. Gradually the people's enthusiasm and affection for hymns will be increased.

• Give hymn backgrounds in service bulletins or by word of mouth. An excellent source for this information is *Hymn Notes for Church Bulletins* by Austin Lovelace. G.I.A. Publications, Inc. $9.00. This can be ordered from the Hymn Society Book Service, Texas Christian University, P. O. Box 30854, Fort Worth, TX 76129. Some sample hymn backgrounds are included in Chapters 3 and 4.

• Copy John Wesley's "Directions for Singing" which are included at end of Chapter 6. Print them in your bulletin and/or glue them onto the flyleaf of the hymnal.

• Install a wall chart lined with rectangles (say 1 by 2 inches) for every hymn

1. A child is born 12/85, 12/88	2. A hymn of glory let us 6/83	3. A mighty for 11/86, 11/87
21. Christ the Lord is 4/85, 4/87, 4/88	22. Christ upon the mt. 6/88, 7/88	23. Christ
41. Earth and all stars 3/87	42. Faith of our 9/86, 4/87	

in the new book beginning with number 1 in the upper left hand corner. Under the hymn title in each square, enter the date of usage of the hymn (e.g. 7/14/ 86, etc.). Thus at a glance you and your people can see which of their favorites are in the book and when they have been used, say, over the past few years. Then as new hymns are introduced, the dates they are sung can be added. Locate this in a hallway where congregation passes frequently. Don't hide it in a corner of the choir room.

• Distribute to the congregation a little booklet of hymns in public domain (non-copyright) which can be used by individuals and families (devotions, sung graces, hymns to be sung while tucking children in bed, family hymn sings). Use your copying machine to make these from either your hymnbook or the *Resource Collection of Hymns and Service Music for the Liturgy* (G.I.A. Publications, Inc.) which contains the words and music for 250 hymns in public domain.

• Tell the folk that there will be opportunity for individuals to purchase the new hymnals not only for use in church but an additional one for use in home.

• Identify two aspects of your task. First, decide what things can be done with the entire congregation in public worship, at church night suppers, and through congregational hymn sings, practices, and festivals. Second, determine what things can be done with smaller groups like ladies' guild, Sunday school classes, and families.

• Preach occasional sermons based on hymns. See Chapter 4.

• Have hymn practices before public worship or at another time. See Chapter 6.

• Plan hymn festivals for your congregation. See Chapter 10.

• Begin a Hymn-of-the-Month program. If you denomination has one, follow its list; if not, select your own hymns. Use each hymn during a month a number of times with various groups and in different ways.

• Help the Christian Education Committee plan greater use of hymns in the church school curriculum including a special class in hymnology. See Chapter 8.

• Dramatize hymns. Stories of hymns contain much material for drama. See, for example, Hal Hopson's *The Singing Bishop* which is a dramatized interpretation of the Palm Sunday hymn "All glory, laud, and honor." It is a delightful children's drama with a small cast of characters, keyboard and optional other instruments, children's or youth choirs and congregation. It is published by the

Chorister's Guild. See Resources at end of book for address of Guild.

• Have choirs sing anthems based on hymns See Chapter 5.

• Purchase books about hymns for your church library. For suggestions see Resources at end of this book. Subscribe to *The Hymn,* a stimulating quarterly journal of The Hymn Society of America.

• Introduce variety in hymn singing in worship. See Chapter 4.

• Invite people to write hymns. Suggest topics and meters and examples.

• Consider the introduction of a cantor into the hymn leadership program. See Chapter 5.

• Introduce frequent use of preludes based on hymn tunes. See Chapter 5 for sources of hymn preludes.

As we said earlier, any of these activities will indicate to the congregation that their musical part in worship is being taken seriously and attempts are being made to help the members grow in skill, understanding, and pleasure.

7. USING DENOMINATIONAL RESOURCES

In deciding procedures for implementing this process, include not only the ideas contained in this book but also utilize printed materials prepared by your denomination to assist in hymnal introduction. They may consist of historical articles in denominational periodicals devoted to the hymnody of your church. Pamphlets give numerous suggestions of methods for introducing the new book and improving congregational singing and probably include a model hymnal dedication service.

You are fortunate if your denomination also issues a companion or handbook for the new book. These books not only include essays about various aspects of hymnology but the main body of the book also presents background information about every hymn in the new book. If your denomination does not have a handbook, buy another denomination's handbook. For list, see Resources at end of book.

Also video and audio cassettes are sometimes available which introduce samples of the hymns in the new book. And some denominational authorities also organize regional and local workshops to give assistance in making full use of the new book.

8. ASSIGNING TASKS

The total task is made much easier and more efficient if the individual projects are farmed out. Here are some possible assignments:

write hymn stories for church newsletters and bulletins

plan hymn festivals

make a careful study of the church's acoustics

work with church school in planning curriculum inclusion of hymns and hymn singing

teach a class on hymnody for adults

direct a hymn drama

study and write history of the congregation's use of hymns

make and maintain the hymn bulletin board.

Assign the implementation of the above projects to committee members and, if needed, recruit other members of congregation to help. Set date for next meeting when the committee can hear reports, assess progress, and plan further steps. Remember that the implementation of these plans falls mainly on the musician and pastor. Therefore weekly conferences between the pastor and musician would be very helpful.

Also develop a job description that spells out the priorities of your musician's duties. During the last generation congregations of this country have increased the number of choirs to be trained by their musicians. Also lately the development of bell choirs has been added to their duties. Be aware therefore that, if you have a series of ensembles (choral and bell), it is time consuming to recruit, rehearse, and direct these groups. This work is valuable but the most important aspect of a church musician's duties is the development of great congregational singing.

Chapter 2
UNDERSTANDING THE RESOURCES
OF YOUR NEW HYMNAL

1. The editing process
2. Overview of the hymnal
3. Page format
4. Indexes

1. THE EDITING PROCESS

When Canon John Julian finished his monumental two-volume *Dictionary of Hymnology* in 1892, he estimated that over 400,000 Christian hymns had been written by that time. By now, almost a hundred years later, the number is closer to a million hymns. Most of these hymns, of course, are inferior and ephemeral, but thousands of them are splendid. Editorial committees have to winnow this mass of hymnody and settle usually upon approximately 600 hymns for the average-sized hymnbook. It has already been pointed out that each denominational choice varies according to its tradition and standards. Lutherans, for example, always include a large number of German chorales. Metrical psalms from Presbyterian and Reformed traditions are emphasized in their hymnals. Methodists feature many of the Wesley hymns. But, as we shall see later, there is an increasing similarity in the content of denominational hymnals.

It will help your committee and your congregation to understand and to make fuller use of the new hymnal if you learn some of the considerations which usually influence editors of various hymnals. Obviously you will learn the specific factors which were considered by the creators of your new book when you read the Preface to your hymnal. Also additional information about your book will be given in articles in your denominational journals and in other publications.

Each generation a hymnal. Denominations issue a new hymnal approximately each generation. This enables the church to have contemporary hymns which express the concerns, the hopes, the new insights as Christians view the world of the present. A high hope in the mind of the Church today is the achievement of permanent peace in a nuclear age. Nowadays we are also concerned as never before with the preservation of the environment. The deepening of the life of the Spirit in all of our members is a constant goal. We note with sadness the increase in poverty and hunger and we need hymns which speak to our duty in alleviating these afflictions. By changing the language of hymns, the editors seek to affirm the participation of all in the body of Christ. There is the celebration of the increasing dialogue between branches of Christendom. The contributions of ethnic, minority, and global churches have found their way into many books.

These are some of the many facets in our new hymnals. Since Webster defines a generation as a span of about 33 years and since many denominations do not care to wait this long to give their members new materials for song, they issue intervening hymnal supplements. Independent publishers also have printed these auxiliary collections.

Familiar and unfamiliar. The task of editors is two fold. First they want to be sure that a sufficient number of familiar, well-loved hymns are retained. They therefore survey what use their denomination has made of hymns in former hymnals and then they determine which hymns should be retained. In preparation for editing a new hymnal, one major denomination queried pastors, musicians, and members for advice on this point. A large majority said they would like for more than two-thirds of such a collection to be familiar to their congregation.

Second, they make a careful study of new hymns to determine which ones should be added. These may be newly written hymns or earlier hymns recently discovered. These are found by research into scores of new hymnals, supplements, and periodicals. Also hymns are commissioned to express an aspect of Christian faith for which there are not sufficient hymns. Also committees receive hundreds of unsolicited hymn texts and tunes. In this process they arrive at what they consider a fair proportion of familiar and unfamiliar.

Historical balance. Just as an editor of an anthology of English literature attempts to present examples of the major writers in this language, so committees try to maintain a balance of hymns from the principal periods of the Church's history. The editors know the long and fascinating story of the church's use of congregational singing and select the classics from the church universal. To give historical perspective, some hymnal handbooks include a chronological index in which its hymns are listed under century groupings.

Singable by congregations. Most editorial committees agree that every hymn should be singable by the people. Also they desire that every musical setting should be playable by a reasonably competent organist or pianist. One hymnal introduction states that its music for congregation "has already been validated as being suited to that idiom. While not every congregation will sing every hymn or type of hymn in this collection, every hymn in this selection has been sung by the people in the pews, some for centuries, some only in the church of the composer for just a few months."* It is true, however, that hymns differ in ease or difficulty of learning and in some hymnals there are hymns which are

---

* *Worship II,* p. iii.

suited mainly for a choir although a congregation with skilled tuition could be taught to master and adopt most of these tougher ones.

Ecumenical hymnody. Because of the increased opportunities for ecumenical dialogue and interdenominational fellowship during the past several generations, hymnal committees keep in touch with each other, share research, and study each other's hymnals. They especially note the list of 227 hymns developed by the Consultation on Ecumenical Hymnody. The index of First Lines in some newer hymnals have asterisks by those hymns which are listed in this ecumenical report. The Episcopal *Hymnbook 1982* includes a separate index of its hymns which are on the Consultation on Ecumenical Hymnody List. See Chapter 3, Section 3 for description of this Consultation.

Two types of hymnals. Your hymnal will probably belong to one of two broad types of hymnals. The first type is restricted to a collection of hymns, usually containing from 400 to 700 hymns with some indexes. Then, in the second type, there are hymnals which contain, in addition to hymns, liturgical material to aid in corporate worship. In simpler form these books carry Scripture passages for unison or responsive reading plus an outline of a service of worship, a few creeds, and musical responses for congregation and choir. Next, there are larger hymnals issued by denominations with a prescribed liturgy. These include not only hymns but also the complete text of the liturgy with musical responses, antiphons, and acclamations printed at appropriate locations in the worship. Sometimes the liturgy with its music is printed in a separate volume and placed in the pew racks along with the hymnal.

Hymnal editions. When the editorial committee has finished the selection of texts and tunes, they must then decide how to present these hymns in book form. Some denominations print just one edition which includes each hymn with full music staff. These books are frequently published also in a spiral binding so that they will lie flat on the organ music rack. Other churches publish not only this full music staff (some call this a choir edition) but they also have a congregational edition with some or all of the hymns having just the melody with the stanzas printed just below the tune. Additional editions include one for instrumental accompaniment, a minister's edition, and an edition with a sizable number of the hymn tunes printed in a lower key. Then for visually handicapped persons a large-print words-only edition in made available. Sometimes this words-only edition is reduced in size so that it is pocket-sized and can be used for private devotional reading.

Handbooks. The hymnal publishers frequently publish a handbook, guide, or companion to accompany their new hymnbook. These are essentially collections of information about each hymn in the book. The handbook gives a narrative about the origin of text and tune, the author and composer, the scriptural background, and other information regarding all of your hymns. Also included may be essays on the history of your denominational hymnody with advice on how to use the hymnal. Buy a handbook of your own hymnal if one is available.

In any event, purchase Austin C. Lovelace's *Hymn Notes for Church Bulletins* (G.I.A. Publications, Inc). It gives brief stories of 400 favorite hymn texts in language aimed at the person in the pew. It is designed to be reprinted, without further permission needed, in church bulletins.

2. OVERVIEW OF THE HYMNAL

Although there are some variations between hymnals, the similarities far outweigh the differences. Most denominational hymnals include the following general sections:

Preface
Table of Contents
Hymns
Service Music
Liturgical Material
Acknowledgements
Indexes

Preface. First, be sure to read this introductory statement. It will tell you the guidelines which directed the editorial committee. If your book is denominationally published, the preface may recount some of the historical background of its hymn singing. Some prefaces add brief essays on the text and music of hymns with instructions as to hymnal use. Also the personnel of the editorial committee may be appended.

Table of contents. This index sets forth in outline form the topical structure of the book. Thorough familiarity with this index will assist leaders of worship to locate hymns dealing with a general topic or a particular liturgical act. For more help in finding specific hymns, there is usually an extensive Topical Index at the end of the hymnal.

Hymns. The largest part of a hymnal is the corpus of hymns. The next section of this chapter describes in some detail the page formats.

Service music. This section includes the shorter musical refrains, acclamations canticles, sung prayers, doxologies, etc. These items are either printed in a section by themselves or are interspersed in the text of the various liturgies. There is considerable variation in this music from church to church. Suggestions for teaching this type of music are given in Chapter 6.

Liturgical material. As said above, most hymnals include some liturgical material. Some denominations include the entire liturgy for the various rites, offices, and services. Since there is considerable difference between denominational liturgies, it is impossible in the scope of this book to deal with them. Your own church provides aids for understanding and using its liturgy.

Acknowledgements. Some books include an index of hymns which are under copyright or are hymns which should have an acknowledgment of ownership and permission to print. Other hymnals place all permission acknowledgments under each individual hymn. This information is important because an increasing number of congregations are including supplemental hymns in their service bulletins. Before printing them in the order of service, the leaders need to know which hymns are in public domain, which are copyright, and where to write for permission to use.

In this connection, attention should be called to *Resource Collection of Hymns and Service Music for the Liturgy* (G.I.A. Publications, Inc.). This book was prepared by the International Commission on English in the Liturgy which is a Joint Commission of Catholic Bishops' Conferences. In it are the texts and full music score of 250 hymns in public domain. These hymns are of high quality and are common to the congregational music of almost every Christian congregation. Any of these can be photocopied in any church bulletin without permission. Also included are copyrighted new hymns and service music along with nine indexes.

Speaking of photocopying hymns, a valuable service is available to local church leaders who want to introduce hymns which are not in their hymnal. It is possible for a fee to secure a license from publishers of hymn texts and tunes. Three leading firms are G.I.A. Publications, Inc., 7404 South Mason Avenue, Chicago, Illinois 60638, Hope Publishing Company, Carol Stream, Illinois 60188, and Hinshaw Music, Inc., P.O. Box 470. Chapel Hill, NC 27514. Permission can be secured on a one-by-one hymn basis or an annual license can be purchased which entitles you to use any hymns from their entire proprietary hymn catalog. Whenever a copyright hymn is printed in your bulletin, the permission notice with license number must be noted under the hymn.

Indexes. The six most common indexes are described later in this chapter.

3. PAGE FORMAT

An understanding of the page format will be of considerable help in a wise use of your hymnal. We will first discuss the display of the hymn itself and then explain the editorial information which surrounds the music.

Hymn display. Although the newer hymnal editors have come up with a variety of modes of displaying the hymn, there are three main ways in general use.

First, the complete music staff is printed with all or most of the text interlined.

The King of Love My Shepherd Is

noth - ing   lack   if   I   am   his   And
where   the   ver - dant   pas - tures   grow,   With
on   his   shoul - der   gent - ly   laid,   And
rod   and   staff   my   com - fort   still;   Thy

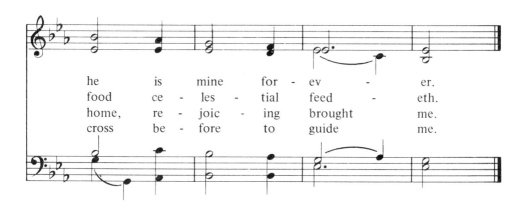

he   is   mine   for - ev - er.
food   ce - les - tial   feed - eth.
home,   re - joic - ing   brought   me.
cross   be - fore   to   guide   me.

5. Thou spreadst a table in my sight;   6. And so, through all the length of days,
    Thine unction grace bestoweth;   Thy goodness faileth never.
And, oh, what transport of delight   Good Shepherd, may I sing thy praise
From thy pure chalice floweth!   Within thy house forever.

Text: Psalm (22)23; Henry W. Baker, 1821-1877
Tune: ST. COLUMBA, 8 7 8 7; Gaelic

This most common mode has the advantage of locating the text next to the music which is full score and can be played as accompaniment. The disadvantage of this display was expressed by W. Thomas Smith, Executive Director of The Hymn Society of America. Speaking of this full score method, he wrote, "Most hymnal formats do not aid the majority, the non-music readers, who are asked to wade through a format which buries the tune in with the accompaniment. . . . It is impossible for the non-reading worshiper to follow the shape of the melody in such an arrangement." Following Smith's reasoning, I favor this full score mode just for the very familiar hymns which require little or no music reading. However, it would help a congregation to tell them that the melody is located in the top notes of the music above the text.

Second, certain hymns are printed with three staves.

1. Let all mor - tal flesh keep si - lence,
2. King of kings, yet born of Mar - y,
3. Rank on rank the host of heav - en
4. At his feet the six - winged ser - aph;

and with fear and trem - bling stand;
as of old on earth he stood,
spreads its van - guard on the way,
cher - u - bim with sleep - less eye,

The accompaniment is in the bottom two staves with the melody only in the top staff. The text is printed under the melody line. Since most of the congregation sing only the tune of the hymn, it is convenient to have this melodic line singled out. Even if the reader is musically illiterate, in time this person may begin to relate the contour of the melody notes to the tune which is being sung. Hymnal editors usually have two reasons for displaying a hymn in this three-staff mode — first, the tune may be exceptionally strong and therefore need a unison rendition, and/or the tune may be brand new and its learning will be facilitated by clearly displaying the melody score. Also folk who want to sing a part other than soprano have the score available.

Third, several major denominations have published pew editions which for all or most of the hymns show only the melody with text just below it.

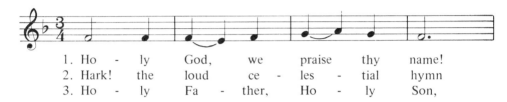

```
1. Ho  -  ly    God,     we     praise    thy    name!
2. Hark!  the   loud     ce  -  les   -   tial   hymn
3. Ho  -  ly    Fa  -  ther,    Ho   -   ly     Son,
```

This method is sensible in that it gives only the essential ingredients of hymn singing — the tune and text. This mode reverts to the way the reformers, Martin Luther and John Calvin, printed their pocket sized hymnals and psalters. It also follows the preference of Dietrich Bonnhoefer who advocated unison singing for his "underground" seminary during the Nazi regime. The denominations which publish the melody-alone edition also have a full score edition (called Choir). Although the melody edition will be in the pews, the congregation should be told that those who read parts (alto, tenor, bass) can be provided with the full harmony edition.

In addition to these three ways, some hymns are printed with a descant, melody in the tenor arrangement (called *faux bourdon*), alternate harmonization, handbell and percussion instruments score, or guitar chords.

Editorial information. There are varieties of ways of displaying information about the text and tune. Chapter 3 includes hymns which are examples of some of these methods. Editors usually place information concerning the text, the music, and performance above or below the music. The name of the hymn is highlighted above the music and this title is usually the first line of the text. The name of the topical grouping such as Advent, Praise of Christ, or Holy Communion is also usually located at top of page.

Information about the text, located ordinarily on the left side, includes the name of the author and sometimes the birth and death dates. Some editors put these dates of authors and composers in the writers' index. If the author is unknown, the name and date of the hymnal or document in which the hymn was first printed is given. If it was written in another language, the name of the translator is added. Also if there is a strong scriptural reference in the text, some editors list the Biblical verse or passage. This is especially true of the Psalms. If the hymn text has been altered, this is usually indicated by the abbreviation *Alt.*

Data regarding the tune, located usually on the right hand, includes its name and the identity of the composer and dates if known. If unknown, the documentary source with date is listed. Frequently these tunes whose origins are unknown are folk melodies which are sometimes called *Traditional.* Also the metrical structure of the tune is added. The use of this valuable bit of information is described later in this chapter in the section on the Metrical Index.

Some hymnals include aids to performance. Certain texts have been associated with several tunes and so, for example, at the bottom of the page you may see this notation *Alternative tune: AUSTRIA 45.* Speaking of alternative tunes, you may occasionally see a hymn text printed with two tunes on adjacent pages. Usually the preferred, and frequently a new and unfamiliar, tune will be printed first. When announcing a hymn with two tunes, be sure to state which one is to be sung.

As an example, the hymn "Jesus, Lover of my soul" was set for years in many American hymnals to the tune MARTYN. Then hymnal editors began including the lovely Welsh tune ABERYSTWYTH alongside MARTYN with this hymn. Now we find some hymnals dropping MARTYN entirely.

If the tune for a particular hymn is used two or more times in the book, the editors sometime set the music in different keys, which means that this music is higher or lower in pitch. So at the bottom of a page you may see a note like this: *For a higher key, see 87.* The editors of a few hymnals (e.g. *Hymnbook 1982* Episcopal) append a metronome number below each hymn to indicate the recommended pace at which the hymn should be played and sung.

4. INDEXES

Although there are almost a score of indexes provided in different hymnals and hymnal handbooks, we will discuss only the ones which are in most books.

1. Table of Contents. Earlier we described this important index which appears at the beginning of hymnals and which describes the broad patterns of topics and uses into which the contents fall.

2. Index of First Lines and Common Titles. All major books include this primary means of finding each hymn in the hymnal. Most hymns are known by the first line. Some, however, have a title like "America the Beautiful" whose first line is "O beautiful for spacious skies." In this case, both names are indexed. The titles are sometimes printed in capitals or bold face type.

3. Tune names. When you sing hymns, make a habit of noting the names of every hymn tune you sing and learn to refer to them by name. Instead of saying, "I like the tune which goes with 'Holy, Holy, Holy, Lord God Almighty' ", say NICAEA. It was given this name because the text deals with the doctrine of the Trinity which was first formally adopted by the Council of Nicaea in A.D.325. Many chorales retain as their tune name the German for the first line. For example, EIN FESTE BURG means "A mighty fortress." Here are several more samples of hymn tune name origins:

Place ABERYSTWYTH. Person BEECHER. Saint ST. PETER.*

One contemporary hymnal tune index includes the first line of the hymn beside each tune name as an aid to identification.

4. Metrical Index. The purpose of this index is to facilitate the exchange of tunes and texts of similar meter. In this index all tunes which fit a particular metrical pattern are grouped together. Alongside the tune name on a hymn page is found a symbol like 87.87.D, CMD. or SM. These numbers and abbreviations indicate the metrical framework of the text. In other words, these numbers tell the exact number of syllables per line or phrase as well as the rhyme scheme. Since the tune of a particular text matches it, it usually means that it is possible, and sometimes desirable, to exchange a text and tune which have the same metrical pattern.

To illustrate, consider the familiar Bishop Ken Doxology, "Praise God from whom all blessings flow." This is called the Long Meter Doxology because Long Meter has eight syllables in each of the four phrases. Count out these phrases on your fingers right now. There are many Long Meter (LM. or 88.88) texts in your hymnal which could easily be sung to the Doxology tune OLD HUNDREDTH. Try these: "Jesus shall reign" and "Where cross the crowded ways of life." Each of these combinations will work. However, some switches are not desirable for reasons which will be mentioned later.

The major use made of this metrical device is to substitute a familiar tune for an unfamiliar one when the leader of worship wants to use a particular text but knows that its tune is unfamiliar and there is not enough time to teach the new tune. This person knows that the people can read and comprehend any English in the hymnal but they may balk quite understandably at a tune they have never sampled before.

Suppose, for example, that you want to use Michael Perry's "Glory be to God

---

* See *Hymn Tune Names,* Robert G. McCutchan, Nashville: Abingdon Press, 1957.

in Heaven" but the people do not know the tune to which it is set in the hymnal and you do not have time to teach it to them. You will see that its metrical signature is 87.87. D. which means that the first line contains eight syllables (count these in its title above). The second line has seven and so on alternating between eight and seven until the end of the stanza. D means doubled (87.87.87.87.) Look down the list of this popular meter in the Metrical Index and try this hymn with a number of familiar tunes. You might settle on the Welsh tune HYFRYDOL or Beethoven's HYMN TO JOY.

A glance at any Metrical Index will reveal this simple arrangement. First are Short Meter (SM. or 66.86) and Short Meter Double (SMD.). Then Common Meter (CM. or 86.86) and Common Meter Double (C.M.D.) are followed by Long Meter and Long Meter Double (LMD.) Then in rising serial order — for example, from 447.76 up to 14.14.478. — tunes in various metrical categories are found. You will also see a section labeled *Irregular* which means that these hymns, while singable, vary in the number of syllables per line in different stanzas. Some examples of this type are "For all the saints" and "God is working his purpose out."

Several bits of advice regarding use of this method of tune interchange should be added. If possible, use the tune given with the text. Follow some of the methods of introducing a new tune which are described in Chapters 3 and 6. It is stagnating to revert to the few old and tried favorites. Next, when seeking another musical setting, adopt one which matches the mood and spirit of the text. One would never think of matching "Joyful, joyful, we adore thee" with the tune CONVERSE which belongs to "What a friend we have in Jesus." (The Scots set "What a friend we have in Jesus" to EBENEZER (the tune usually connected with "Once to Every Man and Nation") in *The Church Hymnary: Revised Edition* 1927!)

Finally, be sure that the accentual pattern of text and tune match. For example, the text "Come, you faithful, raise the strain" and the tune LANCASHIRE "Lead on, O King eternal" are both 76.76. D. but, technically speaking, one is trochaic and the other iambic. In other words, the text has the accent on syllables 1-3-5-7 and the tune throws the accent on syllables 2-4-6. Thus they are incompatible.

Index of Composers, Authors, and Sources. In this index all hymns are listed along with the names of the authors, translators, and sources of words, and according to composers, arrangers, and sources of tunes. Sometimes the birth and death dates of individuals are given in this index unless they have been listed alongside each hymn.

Topical Index. This index lists the hymns under many subject headings. It is a valuable tool for a worship leader needing a hymn to develop a special theme, celebrate an occasion, or express a particular emotion. Earlier in discussing the Table of Contents, I mentioned that hymns are grouped in most hymnals according to subject matter. However, since many hymns have a number of subordinate but important emphases, this index helps locate them. To illustrate, some editors place the familiar hymn "Let all mortal flesh keep silence" in a section called Praise. Other books have this hymn in the section marked Advent or Holy Eucharist. A complete Topical Index will indicate the several emphases present in this and other hymns.

Additional indexes. Here is a list of additional indexes found in various hymnals: Scripture Passages Related to Hymns, Hymns for the Church Year, Liturgical Index, Metrical Psalms and Hymns based on Psalms, Hymns on the Consultation on Ecumenical Hymnody List, Hymns Which May Be Sung in Canon, Psalm Refrains Set to Music, Alphabetical Index of First Lines of All Stanzas, Origin of Tunes — Chronological Listing, Original Language First Lines of Hymns, Index of Hymns by Classification, and Hymns for the Young.

Chapter 3
HOW TO INTRODUCE A NEW HYMN

Several years ago I was asked to lead a hymn festival at a large summer church music conference. I knew that there would be over a thousand choir directors with members of their adult, youth, and children's choirs in attendance. In addition to these musicians, approximately a thousand summer residents at this conference center would also attend.

As I planned the festival contents, it occurred to me that here was a chance to try out a number of the tougher hymn tunes which were not well known in their home congregations. But, knowing their music reading ability, I had little doubt that every hymn I announced would be accessible to them. During the festival I was delighted to hear magnificent hymn singing. There was no hesitance in tackling any of these hymns.

I did not have to *teach* these less familiar hymns. Because the majority of the congregation could read music, they sang with enthusiasm and joy. Since reading music was no problem, they were free to consider the words and to express the ideas and emotions contained in the text.

This experience confirmed my long-held opinion that the primary problem in learning a new hymn is the music, not the words. Except for the very young ones in a local congregation, members have no hesitancy about reading aloud any hymn text, old or new. But, faced with the following hymn which is unknown to many congregations, numerous persons are completely frustrated and unable to sing the tune at sight. If just the melody is printed as in this example, some correlation between text and tune might automatically be made.

Hills of the North, Rejoice

1. Hills   of the North, re - joice,   Ech - o-ing songs a - rise,
2. Isles   of the South-ern   seas,   Sing   to the lis - t'ning earth,
3. Lands   of the East,   a - rise,   He   is your bright-est   morn,
4. Shores of the ut - most West,   Lands of the set - ting   sun,
5. Shout, as you jour - ney   on,   Songs be in ev - 'ry   mouth,

Hail   with u - nit - ed voice   Him   who made earth   and
Car - ry   on ev - 'ry breeze   Hope   of   a   world's new
Greet him with joy - ous eyes,   Praise shall his path   a -
Wel - come the heav'n -ly guest   In   whom the dawn   has
Lo,   from the North they come,   From East and West   and

skies: He   comes in   right -eous - ness   and love, He
birth: In   Christ shall all   be   made   a - new, His
dorn: The   God whom you have   longed   to know In
come: He   brings a   nev - er - end - ing light Who
South: In   Je - sus all   shall find   their rest, In

brings   sal - va - tion   from   a - bove.
word   is   sure, his   prom   -   ise   true.
Christ draws near,   and   calls   you   now.
tri - umphed o'er   our   dark   -   est   night.
him   shall   all   the   earth   be   blest.

Text: Editors of *English Praise*, Based on Charles E. Oakley, 1832-1865, © 1975, Oxford University Press
Tune: LITTLE CORNARD, 6 6 6 6 88; Martin Shaw, 1875-1958, © J. Curwen and Sons

However in the following four part harmony example, it is somewhat harder to locate the melody line unless people have been told where the tune lies.

Hills of the North, Rejoice

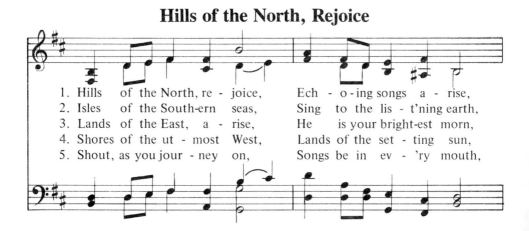

1. Hills   of the North, re - joice,   Ech - o -ing songs a - rise,
2. Isles   of the South-ern   seas,   Sing   to the lis - t'ning earth,
3. Lands   of the East, a - rise,   He   is your bright-est morn,
4. Shores of the ut - most West,   Lands of the set - ting sun,
5. Shout, as you jour - ney on,   Songs be in ev - 'ry mouth,

Hail with u-nit-ed voice   Him who made earth and
Car-ry on ev-'ry breeze   Hope of the world's new
Greet him with joy-ous eyes,   Praise shall his path a-
Wel-come the heav'n-ly guest   In whom the dawn has
Lo, from the North they come,   From East and West and

skies: He comes in right-eous-ness and love, He
birth: In Christ shall all be made a-new, His
dorn: The God whom you have longed to know In
come: He brings a nev-er-end-ing light Who
South: In Je-sus all shall find their rest, In

brings sal-va-tion from a-bove.
word is sure, his prom-ise true.
Christ draws near, and calls you now.
tri-umphed o'er our dark-est night.
him shall all the earth be blest.

Text: Editors of *English Praise,* Based on Charles E. Oakley, 1832-1865, © 1975, Oxford University Press
Tune: LITTLE CORNARD, 6 6 6 6 88; Martin Shaw, 1875-1958, © J. Curwen and Sons

It may be difficult for an experienced musician or minister to understand the stress and even chagrin which a musically illiterate person will feel who is faced with the music score of a brand new tune. Perhaps the following analogy will help.

Suppose that Colossians 3:16-17 is printed in your Sunday morning bulletin. This is the passage in which Paul writes as follows: "Let the message of Christ, in all its richness, find a home with you. Teach each other, and advise each other, in all wisdom. With gratitude in your hearts sing psalms and hymns and inspired songs to God; and never say or do anything except in the name of the Lord Jesus, giving thanks to God the Father through him." (Jerusalem)

But imagine that the clergy had it printed in Greek like this:

ὁ λόγος τοῦ Χριστοῦ
ἐνοικείτω ἐν ὑμῖν πλουσίως· ἐν πάσῃ σοφίᾳ διδάσκοντες καὶ νουθετοῦντες
ἑαυτούς· ψαλμοῖς ὕμνοις ᾠδαῖς πνευματικαῖς ἐν τῇ χάριτι ᾄδοντες ἐν
ταῖς καρδίαις ὑμῶν τῷ ᵇ Θεῷ· καὶ πᾶν ὅ τι ἐὰν ποιῆτε ἐν λόγῳ ἢ ἐν
ἔργῳ, πάντα ἐν ὀνόματι Κυρίου Ἰησοῦ, εὐχαριστοῦντες τῷ Θεῷ
Πατρὶ δι' αὐτοῦ.

Now assume that the minister asked you and the others in the congregation to join in reading it aloud. Probably no persons would be able to pronounce the Greek words, much less know what they were saying. You may be sure that the congregation would let the pastor know in no uncertain tones their annoyance at being asked to participate in a sure fiasco.

This concern of congregations for the music of hymns was underlined in the results of a questionnaire circulated to several thousand members of a main line denomination which was preparing a new hymnal. This representative sampling included church members, officers, pastors, and church musicians from various sections of the country, from rural/urban, small/large, ethnic/minority congregations. One of the questions was the following:

Consider for a moment those hymns that you most enjoy singing. Using the list below, please check ALL of those factors you believe contribute to making those particular hymns enjoyable for you to sing:
poetry of the words   music/melodies   theological content
personal memories/association   rhythm of the music

The most important factor, checked by more than nine of every ten persons in each group, was *the music or melody of the hymn!*

The successful introduction of new hymns is a skill which
is the purpose of this chapter to show how it can be acq
of the congregation, especially the pastor and the musicia
these procedures. With skilled enterprise the people in the
to appreciate and welcome the learning of new hymns. After several preliminary comments, this skill will be described under the following headings:

1 How a church member learns a new hymn.
2 Four principles of learning.
3 What makes a hymn singable?
4 Examples of new hymn introduction.

Before discussing these points, I want to present some ideas.

1. Recognize that God has made a unique gift to us in the art of music. The
Constitution on the Liturgy states, "The music tradition of the universal Church
is a treasure of inestimable value, greater even than that of any other art. The
main reason for this pre-eminence is that, as sacred song united to the words, it
forms a necessary or integral part of the solemn liturgy."[1]

2. Start with the assumption that there is in almost every person a deep spring
of song waiting to be released. Here is a striking confirmation of this hypothe-
sis. A few years ago Alan Villiers was in Cardiff, the capital of Wales. Above
the noise of traffic, he heard the singing of a vast crowd of men. Upon inquiry,
he learned that an international rugby game was about to begin in a nearby
stadium.

> I made for the arena. It was packed, but I found a place in a window of a
> building nearby where I could see and hear. The crowd was singing
> hymns. No cheerleaders — no organization at all. They all just sang per-
> fectly together, as if they had been practicing since birth — 60,000 men,
> mostly in cloth caps, from mine and steel-rolling mill, office, shop, and
> farm, from university and technological college. I felt I was listening to
> the spirit of Wales.[2]

Remember that the Welsh people do not have a monopoly on the joy and skill
of singing. To discover one reason they sing so magnificently, study their hymn
melodies. This music will give guidance to hymn leaders in discovering the meaning
of singability. Analyze especially HYFRYDOL " Come, thou long expected
Jesus," BRYN CALFARIA "God, the Lord, a King remaineth," LLANFAIR
"Christ the Lord is ris'n today," EBENEZER "Once to every man and nation,"
and LLANGLOFFAN "O God of earth and altar."

---

1. Second Vatican Council, December 4, 1963. Chapter VI, #112.
2. From "Wales, Land of Bards," by Alan Villiers, *National Geographic*, June 1965. Used by
permission.

you may not be able to use all of the suggestions given in this and subsequent chapters. Select those ideas which appeal to you and are suited to your talents. Also, after a few months, reread this guide. You may find that some of the suggestions which seemed unusable at first reading are now ones you want to attempt.

4. There are two main occasions on which you can introduce a new hymn to your people. Unfamiliar hymns can be presented in a regular service of worship and also they can be learned (and frequently better) in a more informal occasion of a hymn sing and/or practice. You should use both of them. You will need to decide which of the following suggestions suit a congregational rehearsal and which should be used in a service of worship. Smaller and informal groups can also become acquainted with unfamiliar hymns.

5. A number of the ideas in this chapter will be expanded in the following chapters so be on the lookout for them. For example, Chapter 6 on Congregational Practices will help you to plan a hymn teaching session and to introduce unfamiliar hymns in the service of worship.

6. In public worship there are gradations of success in introducing a new hymn. I am afraid that the most common method is to select an unknown hymn for Sunday morning worship, list it in the service bulletin, and join with the people in trying to sing it. This counterproductive method is almost sure to fail with this particular hymn and over the long range it will put a further damper on congregational singing in general.

A better way is to inform the congregation verbally and by bulletin that the hymn is unfamiliar, urge the people to listen attentively as the hymn is played and the cantor and/or choir sings the first stanza, then join in the singing. It would also help to include, spoken or written, a brief bit of information about the background of the hymn and the structure of the tune. This data could be gotten from your hymnal handbook or from Austin Lovelace's *Hymn Notes for Church Bulletins* (G.I.A. Publications, Inc.)

An additional way would be to have the choir sing the hymn as an anthem the preceding Sunday at which time the people can be encouraged to open their hymnal to this hymn and follow along silently as it is sung by the choristers. This is how John Calvin introduced the brand new metrical psalms and tunes in Geneva. He wrote, "This manner of proceeding seemed specially good to us, that children, who beforehand have practiced some modest church song, sing in a loud distinct voice, the people listening with all attention and following what is sung with the mouth, till all become accustomed to sing communally."*

---

* *Calvin: Theological Treatises.* Vol. XXII, p. 54. (Copyright 1954 by Westminster Press).

The best way would be to set aside occasions for a thorough learning of texts and tunes. Chapter 6 describes hymn practices or rehearsals.

7. A congregation which sings only three hymns on Sunday morning is missing a glorious opportunity to realize the joys and spiritual benefits of singing. This limited use of hymns does not begin to tap the resources in our hymnals. Even if different hymns were sung each Sunday (which heaven forbid), this would cover only 156 hymns a year (52x3). This would be only one fourth of the normal hymnal contents. Other occasions for singing should be provided — informal hymn sings, festivals, practices, singing in homes, church school — to say nothing about increasing the number of hymns sung in Sunday worship.

Many early American hymnals included on the title page these words: "for the public, social, family, and private use of Christians." The editors of these books expected their hymns to be sung on many occasions other than Sunday morning.

8. Whenever a new hymn is being introduced, urge all persons who sing alto, tenor, and bass (ATB) to join with others in singing only the melody. These ATB persons are usually music readers and, unless requested, are apt to sing their non-melody vocal lines, thus depriving the non-readers of useful support as they strive to master a new melody.

9. When is a hymn well-learned? Even if the new hymn has an easily understood text and a singable tune, do not think that it is well-learned by singing it just once. It should be repeated soon. A hymn is well-learned when the entire congregation knows the tune so well that their attention can be concentrated on the text. Recall that the apostle Paul wrote in I Corinthians 14:15: "I will sing with the spirit, and I will sing with the understanding also." You do not expect a novice car driver to look at mountain scenery as he motors along a skyline drive. Only an expert driver can safely steal a glance at the vistas.

As you do some of the above things, you will probably notice that the congregation is developing a growing interest and skill in tackling new hymns.

1. HOW A CHURCH MEMBER LEARNS A NEW HYMN

Since many persons in the pews are illiterate in music matters, what is their response if a brand new hymn is announced? When the organist plays a tune never heard before by the congregation, there is often a negative reaction —

— "Why don't we sing some familiar hymns?"
meaning "I am asked now to sing this text
which I am quite willing to read aloud but this
tune? I have no idea how to read this music! So
I will close the hymnal and my mouth until the
hymn is over!"

This procedure would be like handing an
unrehearsed choir its anthem for the first
time when it files into the choir stalls Sunday morning. The choristers with
embarrassment would muddle through its singing and then sit down with a
sense of failure. This method, when applied to a congregation and its hymns,
is, of course, counter productive.

A person learns a new hymn in two ways — by hearing and/or reading. For
most people the tune is learned by hearing the hymn played and sung a number
of times, perhaps all of his/her life, either at church or at home. Think of your
favorite hymns like "Silent night," "A mighty fortress is our God," "How
firm a foundation," and dozens of others. You probably learned them without
paying much or any attention to the music score. This fact led hymnal editors
of former generations to publish text-only editions. Evidently they assumed
that the congregation had a reserve of memorized tunes to fit all the texts.

Skilled music readers, of course, have a distinct advantage over those who lack
this ability. These readers know how to interpret the notes and to translate this
knowledge into the correct pitch and length of the tones. But even these musically literate persons will soon have salted these tunes in their memory bank
and no longer have to pay attention to the music notation. The optimum solu-
tion to this literacy problem would be to teach the congregation to read music.
This and other chapters will include many suggestions about music reading.*

When teaching a brand new hymn, read or summarize the text. Then work on
the tune. If desirable, you might first let the people concentrate on the notes
alone and have them sing it with a nonsense syllable like *la-la* or *ta-ta*. After
the tune has been partially memorized, then add the text.

Here is a simple instruction which can help the persons in the pews to begin
correlating the music score with what they are hearing from the organ, choir,
and other singers. **Tell the people that the melody is in the topmost notes
above the text.** You will be amazed at how many persons have never known
this. If they have not been noticing the contours of this melody line, urge them

* Chapter 14 "Congregational Rehearsals" of *Hymn & Their Uses,* Sydnor (Agape) gives many
specific directions on how to teach congregations to read music.

to begin doing this, even to the extent of following the notes with their finge
as the hymn is being announced by the cantor/choir and piano/organ. In Section 4 of this chapter I will give some illustrations of ways to introduce specific
new hymns.

2. FOUR PRINCIPLES OF LEARNING

READINESS. Persons need to be prepared for a learning experience whether it
be the subject of ornithology, astronomy, stamp collecting, needlepoint, or
hymn singing. A desire to learn this particular skill or kind of information
needs to be cultivated. Many ways for encouraging interest and skill in congregational singing have already been mentioned and more will follow.

GRADUALNESS. Isaac Watts, the father of English hymnody, had radical
ideas about congregational singing in Britain during the first decades of the
eighteenth century. In the face of a widespread tradition of singing only metrical psalms, he not only wanted to give the English people hymns written from
a Christian perspective (When I survey the wondrous cross) but also he "reno-
vated" the psalter to let it reflect the Christian gospel (Jesus shall reign, Ps.
72). During this revolutionary process his motto was the Latin proverb *Festina
Lente* which means "Hasten slowly. Forward, but not too fast." See Chapter 6
for example of graded introduction of sung psalmody.

In introducing new hymns, this clearly means that a sensible mix of new and
old hymns will be presented. Note also that hymn tunes of good quality vary
considerably in their difficulty or ease of mastery. Therefore unfamiliar hymn
tunes which are easy to sing should be introduced first if your people are not
used to tackling new music. Start with simple melodies and build up to more
difficult ones in order to build confidence.

Sometimes use a new text to a familiar tune, then at a later time teach the new
tune. In the last section of this chapter I grade new hymns from easy to more
difficult.

REPETITION. Since, for many people, learning new hymns involves the
memorization of the new tune, repetition is most important. This is learning by
rote. Remember that even the finest symphony orchestra players need to repeat
their music many times in the learning process. If one is memorizing a poem,
this person needs to repeat the poem, line by line, until it becomes embedded
in the memory.

It is a mistake to introduce a new hymn in one service and then return to it a
year later. It is better to repeat it several time during a brief period. The Hymn

ram is based on this learning principle in that the hymn is
and with various groups in the church during the span of a

PERSEVERANCE. Resolve to continue this program of hymn improvement
indefinitely. When the newness of the hymnal wears off, continue to train and
help your congregation in their praise of God through singing. After all, the
choirs continue to work each week at improving their skills and enlarging their
repertoires. The clergy apply themselves regularly to Bible study and sermon
preparation. The congregation also needs this same steady learning process
with regard to hymns and their uses.

3. WHAT MAKES A HYMN SINGABLE?

One major hymnbook committee adopted the following statement as one of its
guidelines in selecting the contents: "The hymns shall be singable by congregations." What is meant by singable?

People in pews, not musicians, determine what is singable for them. A hymn
tune has to make its own way into the hearts and experience of Christians. It
does not have a public relations agent to accompany it. Tunes like SINE
NOMINE "For all the saints" and CWM RHONDDA "God of grace and God
of glory" have become favorites within the past several generations because
they are *singable.*

Text interpretation. Let's begin by saying, as I have stated a number of times,
that the tune most often determines the singability of a hymn but, before we
discuss the music, we should note that the *text* to some extent affects the ease
of comprehension or singability in the broad context of this word. For example, Isaac Watts, who composed some of the finest hymns and metrical psalms
in the English language, said that he proposed to write down to "the Level of
Vulgar Capacities" which at that time meant that they should be readily under-
stood by the ordinary persons of that day. The continued popularity of his
hymns in all denominations down to the present day attests to the success of
this intention.

On the other hand, several major hymnals include W. H. Auden's poem "He is
the Way." It was not written for congregational singing but as the conclusion of
his longer poem *For the Time Being: A Christmas Oratorio.*

Here is the first stanza the meaning of which cannot be grasped by singing the
hymn once. It must be pondered in relation to the other two stanzas.

He is the Way. Follow him through the Land of Unlikeness;
You will see rare beasts, and have unique adventures.

It is singable, especially with Richard Wetzel's beautiful and flexible setting called NEW DANCE, but it cannot be easily mastered and quickly understood by an ordinary congregation.

The English hymn writer, Fred Pratt Green, wrote the song "Life has many rhythms, every heart its beat" in experimental folk song style. It was sung in Westminster Abbey in 1969 in the very first *Come and Sing* series by pupils in Priors Field School. The seniors wrote to him: "Dear Mr. Pratt Green, We were wondering if you could tell us what these two lines mean from your hymn 'Life has many rhythms'.

'Some who fought injustice added wrong to wrong
Can it be that love is stronger than the strong?'

We want to know because we sing this song a lot as it is one of our favourite songs. Thank you very much." Green comments on this question, "If only all congregations would question the texts of hymns they don't understand . . ."*

2. **Hymn playing and singability.** We should observe also that the singability of a hymn, regardless of quality of music or text, is affected by how the hymn is interpreted and led by the organist/pianist and/or song leader. Many master-pieces of hymn writing are distorted and mutilated by a tempo which is too fast or too slow, by a beat which is irregular and thus unpredictable, and by notes inaccurately played. In other words, such leadership makes hymns almost un-singable. To help in determining the correct tempos, I have placed metronome markings under the hymns included in this chapter. In Chapter 5 I will give specific instructions on the playing and directing of hymns.

3. **Tune anatomy**

We can better understand hymn singability by describing the anatomy of a hymn tune. A comprehension of hymn tune structure will not only help you to select the more singable hymns in your new hymnal but it will also give you clues as to how to present an unfamiliar tune to your congregation in an inter-esting and helpful way. And this insight will help your people venture into new musical territory with eagerness.

A folk melody. Folk tunes are familiar examples of singable music. If they had not been easy to master and recall, they would never have survived. Here are some examples: "Row, row, row your boat," "Frère Jacque," "Here we go round the mulberry bush," and "Three blind mice."

---

* *The Hymns and Ballads of Fred Pratt Green,* p. 11. (Agape)

Let's analyze the last one. The reason "Three blind mice" has been passed on from generation to generation is not only the whimsical text but also a tune with a great deal of thematic repetition. In fact, there are only two themes. The first one is a three-note descending phrase and the second one is a rollicking higher one of nine notes. Let's see how these two bits of music compose this song.

Here is the first three-note phrase. Instead of using music notation, we show the tune by means of lines.

Three

      blind

            mice

The tune begins by repeating the first phrase twice. Try singing it.

The second phrase "See how they run" is also made up of another set of three decending notes but at a higher pitch. Note that the middle note is repeated to take care of the words "how they" Sing this one twice.

See

    how they

         run

The third phrase is longer and is repeated three times to take care of these words:

They all ran after the farmer's wife,
She cut off their tails with a carving knife,
Did ever you see such a sight in your life?

     all ran   farm-
        af-   the
           ter
They   er's wife

The little ditty ends with the words "as three blind mice" sung to the first phrase. Now sing the entire song.

In this song are embodied many of the features which give folk music a universal appeal. You will also find these features in the music of composers like Brahms, Beethoven, Bach, Grieg, and Tchaikovsky. Three of the main attributes are *1. a considerable amount of melodic and rhythmic repetition, 2. a steady beat, 3. an inspired balance between unity and variety.*

Melodic and rhythmic repetition

First, let's discuss melodic and rhythmic repetition. We have seen that "Three blind mice" began with a three-note phrase that was repeated four times. We call the first two identical phrases *exact repetition* because they have the same pitches and note lengths. The second two have the same three descending notes as the first but at a higher pitch. This is called a **sequence.** We also found *exact repetition* in the nine-note phrases which were repeated three times on the same pitches and with the same rhythm.

♭ Steady beat

Second, tap your finger or foot steadily while you sing this song and you will feel the regular beat as if you were walking, skipping, or dancing to your singing.

C Balance between unity and variety

Third, this song illustrates the twin principles of unity and variety which are inherent in all great art. *Unity* was created by repeating the themes — the first one five times and the second one three times — and also by maintaining a regular beat. There is *variety* by changing the pitch when the first theme is repeated the third and fourth time. Also the second theme is completely different from the first theme in its melodic contour, its length, its rhythm, and its pitch level.

Hymn tunes. Now, let's apply some of this information to hymn tunes. Our contention that successful hymn tunes are based on the same principles as folk music is borne out by Erik Routley who wrote:

> Writing music for unmusical people to sing actually amounts to composing folk songs; and it is not surprising to discover how many successful hymn tunes have been composed by ministers of religion. They knew what it was like to stand in a pew and sing. Organists have done it admirably when they too had this remembrance. The person who cannot compose what ordinary people can sing is the musician who, while excellent in any other musical respect, has forgotten or never knew what hymn singing is like for the singer.*

We will use as our first example one of the most widely known melodies in the hymnal — Beethoven's HYMN TO JOY which is derived from the choral section of his Ninth Symphony. On the next page is Henry van Dyke's "Joyful, joyful, we adore you" to which Beethoven's music is usually set in hymnals.

---

* *Church Music and the Christian Faith.* p. 90. Agape: Carol Stream, IL. (Copyright by Agape, 1978. Used by permission.

Joyful, Joyful, We Adore You

1. Joy - ful, joy - ful, we a - dore you,
2. All your works with joy sur - round you,
3. Al - ways giv - ing and for - giv - ing,
4. Mor - tals join the might - y cho - rus,

God of glo - ry, Lord of love; Hearts un - fold like
Earth and heav'n re - flect your rays, Stars and an - gels
Ev - er bless - ing, ev - er blest, Well - spring of the
Which the morn - ing stars be-gan; God's own love is

flowers be - fore you, Open-ing to the sun a - bove.
sing a - round you, Cen - ter of un - bro - ken praise;
joy of liv - ing, O - cean depth of hap - py rest!
reign - ing o'er us. Join - ing peo - ple hand in hand.

Melt the clouds of sin and sad - ness;
Field and for - est, vale and moun - tain,
Lov - ing Fa - ther, Christ our broth - er,
Ev - er sing - ing, march we on - ward,

Drive the dark of doubt a - way; Giv - er of im-
Flow - ery mead - ow, flash - ing sea, Chant - ing bird and
Let your light up - on us shine; Teach us how to
Vic - tors in the midst of strife; Joy - ful mu - sic

mor - tal glad - ness, Fill us with the light of day!
flow - ing foun - tain, Prais - ing you e - ter - nal - ly!
love each oth - er, Lift us to the joy di - vine.
leads us sun - ward In the tri - umph song of life.

Text: Henry van Dyke, 1852-1933, alt., © Charles Scribner's Sons
Tune: HYMN TO JOY, 8 7 8 7 D; Arr. from Ludwig van Beethoven, 1770-1827, by Edward Hodges, 1796-1867

/ = Metronome pulse

Notice that the contours of the melodies in the first, second, and fourth sections are identical until the last measure is reached (Measures are indicated by the vertical lines across the five-line staff.) The second and fourth sections are exactly alike. The last three notes of these two sections bring the melody back to the home tone of the key of G in which this music is written, thus giving a feeling of conclusion. But the first section does not return to this home tone. If you sing this section, you will feel a sense of incompleteness. You want to go on. This is what Beethoven intended. Note, incidentally, that the notes of these three sections move stepwise — no leaps of melody. These three sections with their same first three measures give a powerful sense of unity to the hymn.

Now look at the third section. Variety is added because this section contains new material. There are melodic leaps in the first, second and final measure. Note, incidentally, as you sing or hum the first three measures of this third section that they are very similar to each other.

Beethoven did not write the last section as printed in the above score. Instead of starting this section on the first beat of the measure as was done on the preceding three sections, he locates it just before the bar line, giving the melody an anticipatory and surprising thrust. Two recent hymnals display the last line of HYMN TO JOY with this notation:

Giv - er of im - mor-tal glad-ness, Fill us with the light of day!
Chant - ing bird and flow-ing foun-tain Prais-ing you e - ter - nal-ly!
Teach us how to love each oth - er, Lift us to the joy di-vine.
Joy - ful mu-sic leads us sun-ward In the tri-umph song of life.

So in this masterpiece of melodic writing we see how Beethoven unified and varied his music. By the way, if you would like to see how boring this hymn would be with too much unity, sing the entire first stanza using only the last line of the melody.

Thus far we have been showing how bits or phrases of melody are repeated. We should note also how brief rhythmic patterns are repeated to give cohesiveness to a hymn tune. Here are several rather obvious ones. The tune EBENEZER "Once to every man and nation" has this triplet pattern repeated

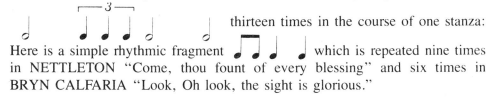

thirteen times in the course of one stanza: Here is a simple rhythmic fragment which is repeated nine times in NETTLETON "Come, thou fount of every blessing" and six times in BRYN CALFARIA "Look, Oh look, the sight is glorious."

Hymn commentators and analyists like to represent the components of tune structure by letters of the alphabet. Since sections 1, 2, and 4 are almost identical we can call them *A* but because sections 1 and 2 are slightly different in the last measure of each, we will call the first section *A*[1] and the second section *A*[2]. The third section, being different, is labeled *B*. So the pattern of HYMN TO JOY is *A*[1] *A*[2] *B* *A*[2].

Many very familiar hymns have tunes with first, second and last lines identical and the third line different. Here are some titles with their tune names:

AABA	Come, thou fount of every blessing	NETTLETON
	All beautiful the march of days	FOREST GREEN
	Once to every man and nation	EBENEZER

There are many other metrical arrangements which give unity and variety to hymn tunes. We will describe some as shown in a few universally loved hymn melodies. The following hymn texts and tunes are included in the list which was developed by the Consultation on Ecumenical Hymnody as guides for editorial committees and for use by local congregations. This Consultation, working from 1968 to 1976, had representatives of thirteen main denominations in America. Their purpose was to determine which hymns are common to our heritage, which hymns should by common consent be retained and which should be "retired" and which tune should be used with each text. The Consultation ended with 227 titles.* Their research and judgment have influenced many recent editorial committees. Granted that the texts of these hymns have high quality, they would not have reached this degree of popular acceptance if they had not been attached to tunes of universal appeal.

Here are twenty of the better known texts and tunes on this ecumenical list. I have chosen these because most readers can hum or sing them from memory and can check the structural patterns to which I call attention. As you read this list, see whether you detect the presence of the three attributes which were listed above:

> *1. melodic and rhythmic repetition*
> *2. steady beat*
> *3. balance between unity and variety.*

   A mighty fortress is our God. EIN FESTE BURG. The melody of the
   first two lines is the same. This is true of many of the German
   chorales.

---

* This list of ecumenical hymns is included in *Hymns & Their Uses* and in *Hymns: A Congregational Study.* James R. Sydnor (Agape: 1982, 1983)

All creatures of our God and King LASST UNS ERFREUEN. AABBC-CBBBBB.

Amazing grace. NEW BRITAIN. Phrases 1,2, and 4 are almost identical. Phrase 3 has two rhythmic bits which are the same.

Come, you thankful people, come. ST. GEORGE'S WINDSOR. The first line is made up of two identical two-measure phrases. Line 3 contains a *sequence*. The second half of this line is the same as the first two measures except at a higher pitch.

Crown him with many crowns. DIADEMATA. Line 3 contains a sequence.

Fairest Lord Jesus. SCHÖNSTER HERR JESU. This folk melody begins with a sequence rising in pitch. Halfway through, at the words "Thee will I cherish, Thee will I honor," we find another sequence, this time descending in pitch.

Glorious things of thee are spoken. AUSTRIAN HYMN. Lines 1 and 2 are the same. Line 3 begins with two five note phrases which have identical time values and almost the same pitches. Line 4 begins with two measures which contain almost an exact sequence.

Guide me, O thou great Jehovah. CWM RHONDDA. The first two measures of the two phrases are identical but take a different tack at the end of each. A musical sequence accompanies the words, "Bread of heaven, Bread of heaven."

Immortal, invisible, God only wise. ST. DENIO. This music is loaded with thematic repetition. Lines 1 and 2 are the same. Line three contains two almost identical bits of melody. The last two measures of line 1, 2, and 4 are the same.

Jesus, lover of my soul. ABERYSTWYTH. Note that the first two-measure up-and-down theme is repeated at the beginning of the first and second line and then concludes the hymn tune.

Joy to the world. ANTIOCH. The text "Let every heart prepare Him room" is set to two downward moving scales which are the same. Then "and heaven and nature sing" is expressed by a descending sequence.

Let all mortal flesh keep silence. PICARDY. AAB. Line one is repeated in line two. The final line is comprised of two almost identical phrases.

O come, all ye faithful. ADESTE FIDELES. The refrain of this familiar carol begins with a sequence.

O little town of Bethlehem. ST. LOUIS. The first and last lines have the same beginning two measures. This same formula applies to the tune AURELIA "The Church's one foundation."

Silent night, holy night. STILLE NACHT. The first four note phrase occurs in four places. See if you can locate them. Notice also the downward sequence with the words "All is calm, all is bright."

Tell me the old, old story. EVANGEL. The verse of the old gospel song is shot through with thematic and rhythmic repetitions and the chorus, which was to be sung by the entire revival congregation, is essentially comprised of three sequences.

The first noel. THE FIRST NOWELL. Thematic repetitions abound in this carol. The two sections of the verse are the same and the refrain quotes from the initial theme.

What child is this. GREENSLEEVES. In the verse of this English folk carol there are two almost identical portions. The refrain likewise begins each line with the same theme but ends differently.

When I survey the wondrous cross. HAMBURG. ABAC

You servants of God. LYONS. Lines 1, 2, and 4 begin with the same five notes and lines 2 and 4 are exactly alike.

4. EXAMPLES OF NEW HYMN INTRODUCTION

Many years ago I introduced a new hymn to a summer denominational conference of about 3,000 people. In preparation for the Sunday evening service I had deliberately told the choir not to come to the choir section of the auditorium because I wanted to let the congregation be the choir. The hymn anthem was "All creatures of our God and King" to the tune LASST UNS ERFREUEN. Although this hymn is widely known now, at that date it had not yet appeared in any of that denomination's hymnals. Therefore few, if any, people had ever heard this hymn. Many of these persons, incidentally, had been raised primarily on a diet of gospel songs.

At this informal service I took about five minutes to teach the hymn. I told the congregation that they were going to be the choir that evening. Then I explained that the text was written by the medieval mystic St. Francis of Assisi who called on all of God's creations to praise God. Next I stated that the hymn tune they were to learn was over 200 years old, having been published in

Cologne, Germany. I mentioned that, although the music on the page looked rather difficult, it was really quite easy to learn since it was composed of three simple musical themes.

I sang the first phrase to them. Then I asked them to join me in singing it. As we sang, I outlined its contour with my hand. I told them that this little snatch of melody was repeated with the next textual phrase. So we sang this. Then we put the first two phrases together. When we had done this, I told them that they had learned one third of the hymn.

Next, holding up my left hand with four fingers extended in view of the people, I told the congregation that the second phrase was a descending row of four notes. I sang it for them, outlining my singing by pointing with my right hand to my left fingers as I sang. They then sang it with me. I told them the next Alleluia was identical. So we sang both Alleluias. "Now you have learned two thirds of the tune," I said.

I then taught them the third phrase in the same manner. The music ends with the theme #2 repeated five times. So I explained that the last part of the melody was the second phrase repeated five times — the first two at a lower pitch, the next two at a higher one (which makes a sequence) and the last phrase returning to the lower pitch but with a *longer* third note. I then sang these five phrases and then requested the people to sing them with me.

Finally with organ accompaniment we had a glorious time standing and singing this famous hymn for the first time. If I had just announced that we were going to sing hymn number 45 "All creatures of our God and King" and asked the people to rise and sing, we would undoubtedly have had a feeble and fumbling attempt on the part of the congregation. As it was, everyone had been instructed and sang eagerly with spirit and understanding. Admittedly, the above occasion was a relatively informal worship at a conference in which this teaching session was appropriate and welcome. Nowadays, incidentally, this tune is frequently sung with the Ken Doxology text, "Praise God from whom all blessings flow."

It should be self evident that the following suggestions for teaching new hymns must be adapted to your particular circumstance and talents. This could be a ten-minute rehearsal before the service begins or at the time for concerns of the church within the worship. A church night supper or a Sunday evening meeting is another possibility. Flexibility of approach is desirable. Chapter 6 on Congregational Practices will also give help.

Remember that you are introducing both text and tune. The meaning of the text can usually be comprehended by the people if they take time to read the words before singing and then concentrate on the text while singing.

If the text is self evident and the tune taxing, give special help in learning the music. In this connection, let's face a basic limitation of the average mind. A person must learn a poem or a piece of music piecemeal. An average congregation cannot memorize a fairly long tune with just one reading or hearing. As an illustration of this problem, I suggest you experiment with Milton's "Sonnet on his Blindness." Here are its fourteen lines:

> When I consider how my light is spent
> Ere half my days in this dark world and wide,
> And that one talent, which is death to hide,
> Lodged with me useless, though my soul more bent
> To serve therewith my Maker, and present
> My true account, lest He, returning, chide;
> 'Doth God exact day-labour, light denied?'
> I fondly ask. But Patience, to prevent
> That murmur, soon replies: 'God doth not need
> Either man's work or his own gifts. Who best
> Bear his mild yoke, they serve him best. His state
> Is kingly. Thousands, at his bidding, speed
> And post o'er land and ocean without rest; —
> They also serve who only stand and wait.'

In an informal hymn sing or practice, before analyzing a new hymn tune, tell the people that you want to try an experiment with them. Tell them that you are

*analogy: learning bib. stories

going to read a few lines of poetry to them and that you want them to repeat these after you. Then read at least the first four lines of Milton's sonnet and ask them to repeat what you have just read. Everyone will probably look at you blankly and say that they can't. Now read them just the first line and ask them to repeat it. Everyone can say it exactly. Then read the second line and ask them to restate it. No problem. If they have opportunity to repeat the lines a number of times, the sonnet could be memorized.

Some of the same problem exists when the congregation is asked to listen to a new and long hymn tune played or sung all the way through. It can be learned this way but you will succeed much faster if you can teach the tune in segments. This is what I described above as I trained the summer congregation to sing "All creatures of our God and King." My motto was "Divide and conquer." Telephone and credit card number designers also divide their codes. They do not give you a string of eleven or sixteen connected numbers. They separate the long numeric codes into sections separated by spaces, parentheses, or hyphens.

This same mode of teaching new hymns was suggested by Sir Walford Davies, former Master of the King's Music in England, who wrote:

> A congregation of good average intelligence and musical ability . . . can soon read a new tune after it is sung or played once. If the conditions are less favorable, a line at a time is a good method. Words and music alike are more thoroughly taught, and the singers kept on the alert, by some such plan as this (with a four-line hymn):
>
> ⌈ First line of verse 1 [the British call a stanza a verse]
>   First line of verse 2
>   Second line of verse 2
>   First two lines of verse 3
>   Third line of verse 1
>   Fourth line of verse 2
> ⌊ The whole of verse 4
>
> This may appear to be fussy, but it works, because it spreads the study beyond the first verse; the repetition of the musical phrase to a fresh verbal phrase is good memory-training; and, above all, it keeps the interest alive.*

We begin with the tune PLEADING SAVIOR which may not be known to your people but is among the easiest to learn. If I were introducing a hymn with this tune in a service of worship or in a hymn practice, I would first make a few

---
* *Music and Worship.* p. 148

comments about the text. Written by Henry van Dyke as a "Hymn of Labor," this is one of the finest hymns on the dignity of work. Van Dyke was the Murray Professor of English Literature at Princeton University. His better known hymn is "Joyful, joyful, we adore Thee."

Next I would explain that, although in many hymnals the hymn tune has four lines, it has so much repetition that the people need learn only a line and a half. The first, second, and last lines are identical and the third line is comprised of two almost identical sections. Incidentally, the tune of the first measure is repeated six times within a stanza.

I would sing the first line in its entirety and then ask the congregation to sing it with me. Then, having told them that this musical phrase also fits the words of the second line, I would have them sing this line with me. Now we would tackle the third line. I would illustrate how it is comprised of two almost identical phrases. Now we would sing this line and then put the hymn altogether by singing an entire stanza. If you do this, you will probably find them joining enthusiastically with you and having a nice inward glow of accomplishment.

Incidentally, in teaching this folk hymn to your congregation, you may want to explain that this tune is built on the pentatonic scale which is the basis for many folk melodies throughout the world. For further explanation of this five-note scale, see page 92.

Jesus, Thou Divine Companion

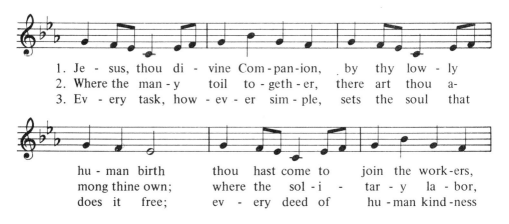

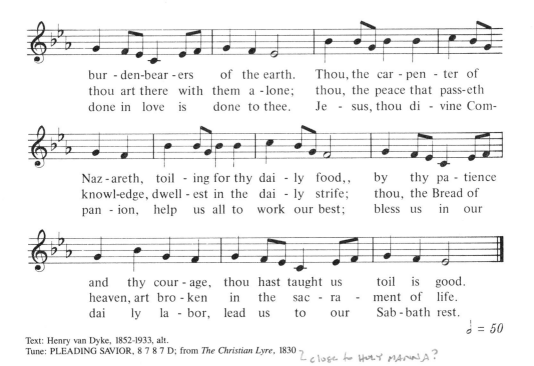

bur - den-bear - ers   of the earth.   Thou, the car - pen - ter of
thou art there with them a - lone;   thou, the peace that pass-eth
done in love is   done to thee.   Je - sus, thou di - vine Com-

Naz - areth, toil - ing for thy dai - ly food,,   by   thy pa - tience
knowl-edge, dwell - est in the dai - ly strife;   thou, the Bread of
pan - ion, help   us all to   work our best;   bless us   in our

and   thy cour - age, thou hast taught us   toil is   good.
heaven, art bro - ken   in   the   sac - ra - ment of life.
dai   ly   la - bor, lead us   to   our   Sab - bath rest.

$\text{♩} = 50$

Text: Henry van Dyke, 1852-1933, alt.
Tune: PLEADING SAVIOR, 8 7 8 7 D; from *The Christian Lyre,* 1830 ⸗ *close to HOLY MANNA?*

PLEADING SAVIOR seems never to have found a single textual mate in our denominational hymnals. Each of five recent hymnals includes it but employs a different text:

Jesus, thou divine Companion
All the way my Savior leads me
Hail, thou once despised Jesus
Sing of Mary, pure and lowly
Lord, with glowing heart

After you have taught PLEADING SAVIOR, you may taste some of the same satisfaction that was experienced by Herbert Wiseman who had conducted congregational practices in numerous Scottish churches. He remarked, "The congregations varied in composition, but in most cases they have been alike in showing an attitude of doubt at the beginning and of enthusiasm at the end of the practice."* This has been my experience without fail.

There are many excellent hymn tunes being written today and some of these are destined to become classics in congregational repertoire. Most editors are including these and thus giving them a chance to be tested by congregations.

* *Manual of Church Praise according to the Use of the Church of Scotland.* p. 150.

The people themselves will ultimately determine which are ephemeral or lasting.

I have chosen the following six hymns as ones which I foresee entering the ecumenical repertoire and having a good chance of survival. I will begin with ones which I consider simpler to learn and move toward the more difficult. I have kept my comments brief. When you teach them, you may want to include more or less information and to take a completely different approach in your tuition. Please note the metronome markings.

Jesu, Jesu, Fill Us With Your Love

Refrain
Unison

Je - su,   Je - su,   fill   us with your love, show

us how to serve   the neigh-bors we have   from   you.

1. Kneels at the feet of his   friends,   si - lent - ly wash - es their
2. Neigh - bors are rich   and   poor,   neigh-bors are black, brown and
3. These   are the ones we should serve,   these are the ones   we should
4. Lov - ing puts us   on our   knees,   serv - ing as though we   are
5. Kneel   at the feet of our   friends,   si - lent - ly wash - ing their

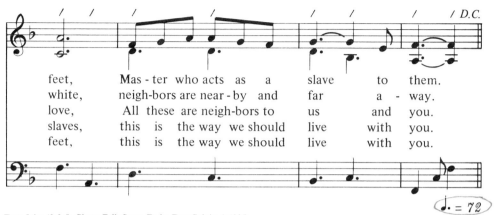

feet,   Mas - ter who acts as   a   slave   to   them.
white,   neigh-bors are near - by and   far   a -   way.
love,   All these are neigh-bors to   us   and   you.
slaves,   this is the way we should   live   with you.
feet,   this is the way we should   live   with you.

Text: John 13:3-5; Ghana Folk Song; Tr. by Tom Colvin, b.1925
Tune: CHEREPONI, Irregular; Ghana Folk song; Acc. by Jane M. Marshall, b.1924, © 1982, Hope Publishing Co.
© 1969, Hope Publishing Co.

Here is a Ghana folk song which exhibits the three elements of folk music
discussed earlier: 1. Pitch and rhythmic repetition, 2. Steady beat, 3. Balance
between unity and variety. The refrain is at the top of the page with the five
stanzas underneath. The refrain begins with an upward leap of two notes and is
followed immediately by a downward leap on these same two pitches. This is
followed by three sequences. The stanzas below are likewise set to a melody
which is simply three sequences. A very learnable tune.

As the Bridegroom to His Chosen

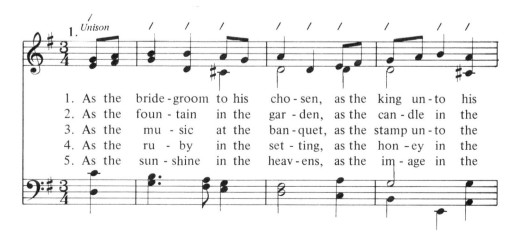

1. As the   bride - groom to his   cho - sen, as the   king un - to   his
2. As the   foun - tain   in the   gar - den, as the   can - dle in   the
3. As the   mu - sic   at the   ban - quet, as the   stamp un - to   the
4. As the   ru - by   in the   set - ting, as the   hon - ey in   the
5. As the   sun - shine   in the   heav - ens, as the   im - age in   the

Text: John Tauler, 1300-1361; Para. by Emma Frances Bevan, 1827-1909
Tune: BRIDEGROOM, 8 7 8 7 6; Peter Cutts, b.1937, © 1969, Hope Publishing Co.

♩ = 88

The above remarkable text by the German mystic, John Tauler, has twenty metaphors for Jesus. The Englishman, Peter Cutts, one of the finest hymn tune composers of the present day, wrote this tune BRIDEGROOM. Its form is simple — three sections, the first two of which are almost identical sequences. The final phrase "So, Lord, art thou to me" is imaginatively set by an antici-patory rhythm on the word "So." Do not neglect to let the congregation hear the beautiful harmonic support for this lovely melody. It is very easy to learn.

The author of the next hymn, Brian Wren, heads it with these words: "The church taking stock of itself." John Wilson, another Englishman, composed the music whose first two lines are in two measure groupings. The second line has a rising sequence. The music has two unique ideas at the end. First, there are two endings. Second, he concludes the melody on a high note (the fifth in the scale) whereas most hymns conclude with the low note of the scale.

We Are Your People

1. We are your peo-ple: Lord, by your grace,
2. How can we dem-on-strate your love and care—
3. Called to por-tray you, help us to live
4. Glad of tra-di-tion, help us to see
5. Joined in com-mun-i-ty, break-ing your bread,
6. Lord, as we min-is-ter in dif-ferent ways,

you dare to make us Christ to our neigh-bors
speak-ing or lis-tening? bat-tling or serv-ing?
clos-er than neigh-bors, o-pen to strang-ers,
in all life's chang-ing where you are lead-ing,
may we dis-cov-er gifts in each oth-er,
may all we're do-ing show that you're liv-ing,

of ev-ery na-tion and race.
help us to know when and where.
a-ble to clash and for-give.
where our best ef-forts should be.
will-ing to lead and be led.
meet-ing your love with our praise.

Text: Brian Wren, b.1936, © 1975, Hope Publishing Co.
Tune: WHITFIELD, 5 4 5 5 7; John W. Wilson, b.1905, © 1980, Hope Publishing Co.

♩ = 88

Creating God

1. Cre - a - ting God, your fin - gers trace the
2. Sus - tain - ing God, your hands up - hold earth's
3. Re - deem - ing God, your arms em - brace all
4. In - dwell - ing God, your gos - pel claims one

bold de - signs of far - thest space; let sun and moon and
mys-t'ries known or yet un - told; let wa - ter's fra - gile
now de - spised for creed or race; let peace de - scend - ing
fam - ily with a bil - lion names; let ev - ery life be

stars and light and what lies hid - den praise your might.
blend with air, en - a - bling life, pro - claim your care.
like a dove, make known on earth your heal - ing love.
touched by grace un - til we praise you face to face.

♩ = 58

Text: Jeffery Rowthorn, b.1934; © 1979 by The Hymn Society of America
Tune: KEDRON, LM; Pilsbury's *United States Harmony*, 1799

"Creating God, your fingers trace" was written by Bishop Jeffery Rowthorn, The opening two words of each stanza indicate that that stanza defines an attribute of God — Creating, Sustaining, Redeeming, or Indwelling. Since this hymn is a prayer, it might be a good idea on the Sunday preceding the introduction of this hymn to have the people read this text as a congregational prayer, telling them that it will be sung next Sunday.

A splendidly constructed minor melody, it should be sung in unison. The rhythmic segments are constructed of quarter and half notes with four dotted notes for variety. Sections 1 and 2 begin with the same four notes. Have the choir sing this hymn the preceding Sunday in anthem form, being sure to call the people's attention (verbally and in the bulletin) to its location in the hymnal.*

If appropriate, the congregation might be told that KEDRON is an old folk hymn melody. It was first published in Amos Pilsbury's *The United States' Sacred Harmony,* 1799. This book is one of the earliest known tune books to contain authentic folk hymns. Pilsbury was a singing master active in Charleston, South Carolina. The composer of KEDRON is unknown. This was one of the most popular tunes in pre-Civil War days in the rural south.

****

The next hymn, "Ye who claim the faith of Jesus" is based on the Annunciation and Visitation of Mary. Stanza 4 is a versification by F. Bland Tucker of the *Magnificat.*

This musical setting by David Hurd has many admirable features. The melody is eminently singable, being divided into three sections marked by numbers. The rhythmic pattern of each section is identical. When you study this music, by all means first sing and play the melody without accompaniment. Next, notice that the keyboard introduction announces the rhythmic framework of each section and intimates the melody. When you add the harmony, you will appreciate its freshness. Finally the descant with the Latin *Magnificat anima mea Dominum* adds a halo to the music.

In singing any of these multi-stanza hymns, consider utilizing the custom of alternation which is described in Chapters 4 and 6. In brief, it means assigning different stanzas to various groups of singers: choir/congregation, men/women, left/right sides of the aisle, and so on.

---

* "Creating God, your fingers trace," Set by Walter L. Pelz as a Hymn Concertato for Mixed Choir, Flute, Congregation and Organ. Agape, HSA 104. Commissioned by The Hymn Society of America

Ye Who Claim the Faith of Jesus

Introduction/Interlude

Descant

4. "Mag - ni - fi - cat

1. Ye who claim the faith of Je - sus, sing the
2. Bless-ed were the cho-sen peo - ple out of
3. There-fore let all faith-ful peo - ple sing the
4. "Mag-ni - fy, my soul, God's great - ness; in my

an - i - ma me - a

won - ders that were done when the love of God the
whom the Lord did come; bless-ed was the land of
hon - or of her name; let the Church, in her fore-
Sa - vior I re - joice; all the a - ges call me

Text: Vincent Stuckey Stratton Coles, 1845-1929, alt.; St. 4, F. Bland Tucker, 1895-1984
Tune: JULION, 8 7 8 7 8 7; David Hurd, b.1950, © 1983, GIA Publications, Inc.

♩ = 78

Now the Silence

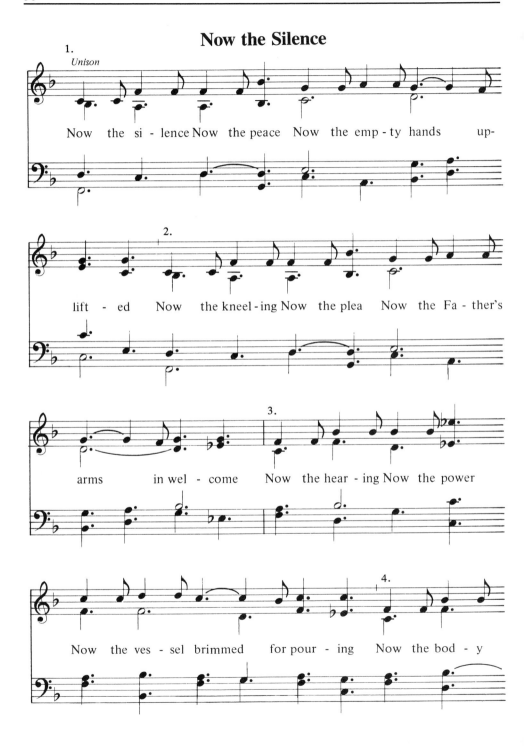

Now the si - lence Now the peace Now the emp - ty hands up-

lift - ed Now the kneel - ing Now the plea Now the Fa - ther's

arms in wel - come Now the hear - ing Now the power

Now the ves - sel brimmed for pour - ing Now the bod - y

Now the blood   Now the joy - ful cel   -   e - bra - tion

5. Now the wed-ding Now the songs Now the heart for - giv - en leap-ing

6. Now the Spir - it's vis - i - ta - tion, 7. Now the Son's e -piph - a - ny,

8. Now the Fa - ther's bless - ing   Now   Now   Now

Text: Jaroslav J. Vajda, b. 1919
Tune: NOW, 4 3 8 4 3 8 D with refrain; Carl Schalk, b.1929
© 1969, Hope Publishing Co.

♩. = c. 60

"Now the silence," written in 1969, has quickly found its way into most significant hymnals since it was first published. Two Lutherans collaborated in creating this masterpiece: pastor/hymnwriter Jaroslav Vajda and music professor Carl F. Schalk. It is singular because it has just one stanza. The word "Now" appears 21 times. It describes and evokes a feeling of mystery and awe of the Christian at Holy Communion.

Eighteen years later Vajda wrote this stanza expressing the bliss of eternal life.

Then the glory
Then the rest
Then the sabbath peace unbroken
Then the garden
Then the throne
Then the crystal river flowing
Then the splendor
Then the life
Then the new creation singing
Then the marriage
Then the love
Then the feast of joy unending
Then the knowing
Then the light
Then the ultimate adventure
Then the Spirit's harvest gathered
Then the Lamb in majesty
Then the Father's Amen
Then Then Then.*

The music NOW is a perfect means of evoking the emotion of the text. It will be of considerable help in teaching this unusual melody to have a clear understanding of its structure. All of the following analysis does not have to be explained to the congregation but it should suggest modes of introduction. The code for Schalk's structure might be indicated AABBA with the last A diversified. The eight sections are identified by a number above the score.

Sections 1 and 2 constitute AA and the melody is exactly the same in each. Sections 3 and 4 are BB and likewise are identical in pitch and rhythm. Note, however, that A and B have the same melody but B is at a higher pitch, thus making it a sequence. Section 5 is exactly like number 1 except for the higher

---

* Words copyright 1987 by Hope Publishing Company, Carol Stream, IL 60188. Used by permission.

note on the word "heart." Schalk shows his ingenuity in developing sections 6-8. Instead of going back to the beginning of section 5, he quotes only the latter part of this theme and he does it in each of these three sections. He draws the music to a serene conclusion by going from the quarter/eighth note rhythm to dotted quarter notes and then two dotted half notes, and a held dotted quarter.

The entire melody is punctuated gently by a steady beat which should be about M.M. ♩. = 60 . There is a reiteration of the quarter/eighth note triple rhythm in most of the melody but Schalk preserves the freshness by inserting dotted quarters and especially by extending the seventh beat in sections 1-5 by using a dotted quarter tied to another quarter. The careful spare harmony ideally supports the melody.

If this hymn is not in your hymnal, license to reproduce it can be secured from the publisher, Hope Publishing Company, Carol Stream, IL 60188.

Part Two

HOW TO IMPROVE
CONGREGATIONAL SINGING

A. The Leadership of Congregational Singing
Chapter 4
CLERGY AND THE USE OF HYMNS

Sir Wilfred Grenfell, medical missionary to Labrador, was traveling with dog team and medical supplies across a frozen bay when his sled plunged through the ice. He managed to drag the dogs onto an ice pan. Partially snowblind and frozen, floating out to sea, he said that he had no sense of fear, that he was upheld by the words of an old hymn which, he said, "quite unbidden, kept running through my head:

> My God and Father, while I stray
> Far from my home in life's rough way,
> O teach me from my heart to say,
> 'Thy will be done,' "[1]

Natives on high cliffs in the distance saw Sir Wilfred and rescued him.

James Muilenburg, former Professor of Hebrew at Union Theological Seminary in New York City, wrote of the "continuing influence of the great hymns of the Church. It would not be difficult to speak of my spiritual pilgrimage in the language of the great hymns."[2]

Phillips Brooks, noted preacher of the last century, was taught as a boy to memorize new hymns and recite them for the benefit of his family each Sunday. By the time he entered Harvard, he is said to have known two hundred by heart.

The German theologian, Dietrich Bonhoeffer, found his terminal days in the Nazi Tegel prison in Berlin more bearable because of hymns. He wrote to his parents, "What a great comfort Paul Gerhardt's hymns are! I am learning them off by heart."[3] He had sung Gerhardt's hymns since childhood.

And Paul, the apostle and pastor, had memorized hymns. He and Silas sang some at midnight in the Philippian jail. He quoted several in letters to his churches. Also he tells how he sang: "I will sing with the spirit, and I will sing with the understanding also." (I Cor. 14:15)

---

1. *The Story of a Labrador Doctor.* London: Hodder & Stoughton, Ltd. p. 217.
2. *Union Theological Quarterly Review.* Vol. XVII, No. 4. May, 1962. p. 292. Union Theological Seminary in the City of New York.
3. *Letters and Papers from Prison,* Edited by Eberhard Bethge. Translated by Reginald H. Fuller. p. 28. London: SCM Press, 1953.

These are five examples of pastors who sang, read, memorized, and depended upon hymns. I urge you to emulate them. Keep your personal copy of the hymnal on your bedside table or next to your reading chair. Absorbing the texts of many great hymns will assist you to enjoy in your life much of the devotion and spiritual insights of the writers of hymns. Memorization of the choice ones will aid you in your private and public prayers and will become a part of your pastoral vocabulary. Also this private acquaintance with hymns will be the starting point for your leadership in a widening use of hymns by your flock.

In addition to reading hymns, learn about the origin of hymns. A minister friend of mine has made it a custom each week to read the stories of the hymns chosen for the following Sunday morning service. He did not give all of this information to the congregation each Sunday but he built up a wealth of personal knowledge. His congregation caught a great deal of his zest for hymns. Dr. Frederick Gilman expresses the value of this knowledge as follows:

> A hymn book is a transcript from real life. The heart of the Christian Church is revealed in its hymns; and if we will take the trouble to relate them to the circumstances that gave them birth, we shall find that they light up with a new meaning and have fresh power to help us in our daily lives.

A good source for this information is your denominational hymnal handbook. The list of Resources at end of this book gives the titles to hymnal handbooks or companions.

This entire book *Introducing a New Hymnal* is designed for pastor's reading. Although this particular chapter is devoted to the specific role of clergy, the other chapters in this guide give important help. I urge you to read all of them carefully. Chapter 1 highlights the part which pastors play in formulating the strategy to be followed in introducing a new hymnal. Chapter 2 describes how to understand and use the resources of the hymnal. And Chapter 3 explains how to introduce a new hymn. The other chapters also present ideas which will help pastors.

This chapter contains the following sections:

1 Why we use hymns
2 Choice of hymns
3 Chancel/pulpit leadership
4 Hymn sermons
5 Pastoral and educational use of hymns
6 Alternative ways of singing hymns

1. WHY WE USE HYMNS

Christians use hymns because through hymn singing

— they express their feelings and ideas,
— they can tell others what they believe,
— they are bound in closer fellowship,
— they are instructed in the fundamentals of their faith, and
— they are sustained in daily life.

2. THE CHOICE OF HYMNS

A controlling principle in hymn selection is that the hymn should capture and express the thoughts and emotions of the congregation in the action of the liturgy. This choice is governed by what happens before and after the particular hymn.

Here are some of the factors which affect hymn selection:
* the familiarity of hymn
* the master plan for introduction of new hymns
* the relation to the theme of the worship
* the Church Year and Lectionary

Familiarity. In selecting a particular hymn, it is wise to consider whether it is unknown, partially known, or familiar. Sensible introduction of a new hymnal requires a carefully balanced schedule of familiar and unfamiliar. Regardless of a hymn's appropriateness for the movement of the liturgy, if the people have not seen the hymn before, it may completely lose its effectiveness. A new hymn should not be introduced into worship until the congregation has been taught it; then the people are freed to pay attention to the text.

Master plan. In Chapter 1 we said that it is a good idea to draw up a master list of new hymns to be introduced over the next several years. Many pastors plan the worship services and their hymns for three months ahead. This enables the organist/pianist to learn the notes, the choirs to master these hymns in their rehearsals, and the congregation to have practice in singing these hymns.

Theme of worship. In non-liturgical churches, worship centers on a theme, sometimes dictated by the sermon topic. In these services, the opening hymn is almost always a hymn of praise or a metrical psalm. The remaining hymns are related to the particular lection(s), the sermon, and the need for an act of dedication at the conclusion.

As explained in Chapter 2, the Table of Contents will give immediate direction toward the broad group of hymns in each category of topics. Then for more precise focusing on a theme, consult the Topical Index. To secure further correlation between scripture readings, sermons, and hymns, many hymnals include an Index of Scriptural References. The Hymn Society of America has published an *Index of Biblical Characters in Hymns,* compiled by Judy Hunnicutt, which is helpful when planning a worship service emphasizing a particular Biblical character. See Resources at end of book for address of Hymn Society.

Church year and Lectionary. In varying degrees churches observe the Christian Year and utilize the Lectionary developed by the International Consultation on English in the Liturgy. Some hymnals include indexes of hymns for these lections and seasons which inform and express the thoughts and emotions for that Sunday. Several denominations sing a *de tempore* hymn which is the name given to the chief hymn in the service on every Sunday and festival, so called because it fits the specific day and season in the church year and responds most intimately to the dominant theme of the day, which is usually contained in the Gospel for the day.

****

I urge you to be involved in hymn selection. Do not turn this important task over to your musician or some other person. Set up a weekly staff conference. Consult your musician in hymn selection not only about the tune but also the text. This person can advise about the familiarity of the text and tune and, if several tunes are given, can help decide which one to use. If it is feasible to select another tune, you and the musician can consult the Metrical Index to find an appropriate substitution.

Many ministers keep a record of the choices by writing the date of use in the margin of their personal copy of the hymnal or in a notebook which can be passed on to their successor. Chapter 1, Section 6, has a description of a bulletin board method of keeping track of hymn use.

Some ministers involve their people in hymn selection by having them list their ten favorite hymns. Then from time to time, when appropriate, the pastor can use these, announcing that a hymn is taken from the list of the people's favorite hymns.

Selecting stanzas

In well-wrought hymns, stanzas are connected logically with each other and consequently, as a rule, the entire hymn should be sung. If it seems wise and necessary to shorten a hymn, care must be used in stanza selection. Some hymns like "Come, thou almighty King" (based on the Trinity) and "The King of love my shepherd is" (based on the 23rd Psalm) should not be abbreviated. Care should be taken in selecting those stanzas which, if omitted, do not violate the sense of the hymn. Some editors help in this matter by placing an asterisk by those stanzas which can be omitted.

Use of hymn fragments

Obviously entire hymns are usually sung in worship. However an increasing number of churches are singing just a single stanza at suitable places in the worship. For example, there are many stanzas (usually the concluding ones) which are ascriptions of praise to the Trinity. These stanzas can express praise and thanksgiving after the declaration of pardon or at the presentation of the offering or as acclamations at appropriate times. An index of doxological stanzas is given in some hymnals, one of which lists almost one hundred hymns with these trinitarian doxologies.* During World War II one congregation each Sunday sang just the first stanza of "O God of love, O king of peace, make wars throughout the world to cease" immediately preceding the benediction.

Numerous congregations sing fragments of stanzas. For example, these lines from familiar hymns enable congregations to utter a brief affirmation of praise:

From "For the beauty of the earth"

Lord of all, to   thee we raise   this our hymn of grate-ful praise.

From "Good Christian friends, rejoice and sing"

Al-le-lu-ia,   al-le-lu-ia,   al-le-lu-ia.

In Chapter 6, Service Music section, there are more examples of snatches of hymns used as refrains including a descant for the Alleluias quoted above.

---

* *Lutheran Worship.* The Lutheran Church — Missouri Synod 1982. p. 1005. Concordia Publishing House.

3. CHANCEL/PULPIT LEADERSHIP

Chancels and pulpits are so situated that the leader is the focus of all eyes as they are raised frequently from the hymnals. If the worshipers see a leader who is enjoying singing, they are stimulated to do likewise. This subtle, though powerful, pulpit influence on hymn singing cannot be overemphasized.

Nowadays the advent of copying machines has made it possible to print and distribute orders of service. Although these worship bulletins make it practicable to present much liturgical material, they have tended to keep the worship leader from making any personal comment about a particular hymn. I am not suggesting that every hymn needs a verbal announcement but, in my opinion, it is occasionally appropriate and helpful to give some background and encouragement.

I recall worshiping in a liturgical church when the rector made this announcement:

> Our hymn is "The spacious firmament on high." The text was written by the English essayist Joseph Addison who based it on the 19th Psalm, "The heavens declare the glory of God." The music is taken from Joseph Haydn's oratorio *The Creation*. Since the music is unfamiliar to many of you, I suggest that you listen carefully as the organist plays through the hymn and the choir sings the first stanza. Then please rise and join in singing the remaining stanzas.

If the hymn is "Joyful, joyful, we adore thee," you might stimulate the people to concentrate on the text by saying,

> The next hymn was written by Henry van Dyke who was visiting in the home of the president of Williams College which is located in the beautiful Berkshire mountains in northwest Massachusetts. Impressed by the majesty of the mountains and the loveliness of the countryside, he wrote "Joyful, joyful, we adore thee" and handed the words to his host saying "Here is a hymn for you. Your mountains were my inspiration. It must be sung to the music of Beethoven's 'Hymn to Joy.'"

Of course, this information can be printed in the bulletin but, occasionally, it is encouraging to have leaders of worship in their own words give some insights into hymns.

4. HYMN SERMONS

Certain hymns are closely related to scripture passages and can serve as a basis for sermons. For example, the apostle Paul quoted a hymn in Philippians 2:6-11 which pictures Christ as the Servant. It has been paraphrased in poetic form in the following two hymns: "At the name of Jesus" by Caroline M. Noel and "All praise to thee, for thou, O King divine" by F. Bland Tucker. If your sermon is based on this scriptural passage, you might incorporate one or both of these hymns in its structure.

The doctrine of prevenient grace (grace operating on one's will before one turns to God) is clearly and beautifully expressed in this hymn, the first stanza of which is:

> I sought the Lord, and afterward I knew
> he moved my soul to seek him, seeking me;
> it was not I that found, O Savior true;
> no, I was found of thee.

John Newton expresses this same doctrine in his autobiographical hymn "Amazing grace" when he wrote:

> 'Twas grace that taught my heart to fear,
> and grace my fears relieved;
> How precious did that grace appear
> The hour I first believed.

For a sermon on prayer, Bishop Thomas Ken's evening hymn "All praise to thee, my God, this night" is an excellent example of the pattern of prayer. Beginning and ending with the note of praise, its others stanzas include confession and petition.

Some pastors have preached sermons with hymns inserted at appropriate points. For instance, one minister preached a sermon based on Psalm 130 in which the stanzas of Martin Luther's hymn "Out of the depths" were sung to illustrate the movement of the psalm.

Another pastor preached a sermon in which he used these spirituals to illustrate the events leading up to the crucifixion and resurrection of Christ:

> When Israel was in Egypt land   Let us break bread together
> Go tell it on the mountain   Were you there
> There is balm in Gilead

The reporter of this event wrote: "The congregation sang better, perhaps because they were involved in the making of a sermon and the establishing of theological connection between hymns."

(I don't follow the sequence chosen, but I like the idea.)

5. PASTORAL AND EDUCATIONAL USE OF HYMNS

Hymns are pastoral aids. A minister entered a hospital room where a young lady lay desperately ill, seemingly unconscious. He stood by the bed for a few minutes, then spoke these lines from a familiar hymn, "Be not dismayed what-e'er betide, God will take care of you." Some weeks later, this lady, now on the road to complete recovery, told her pastor that she had heard and under-stood his reassuring words. They were, she felt, the turning point in her ill-ness.

Suggest that your congregation spend some time during the prelude reading the hymns listed in the order of service. Louis F. Benson said: "It is only the precedent appropriation of the hymn's message by each individual heart that makes its congregational singing worthwhile."*

A publisher of an important denominational hymnal highlighted his promo-tional brochure as follows: "The hymnbook that must be READ to be appreci-ated."

To stimulate your people in developing the habit of memorizing hymns, try this method. A pastor prepared a bulletin insert which had the text of three hymns. The heading was *Try memorizing the following hymns.* Then he copied Bishop Thomas Ken's morning hymn "Awake, my soul, and with the sun" and his evening hymn "All praise to thee, my God, this night" introduced by this sentence: "The following two hymns were written in 1674 by Thomas Ken for the boys of Winchester College where he was chaplain. Each concludes with the familiar Doxology."

Next, he printed the text of "If thou but suffer God to guide thee" with these words of explanation:

> The following hymn was written by Georg Neumark in Germany during the Thirty Years War (1618-1648). While on his way to a university with a group of travelers, he was robbed of all his possessions. He managed to find employment as tutor in the home of a judge. Neumark expressed his joy as follows: "which good fortune coming suddenly, and as if fallen from heaven, greatly rejoiced me, and on that very day I composed to the honour of my beloved Lord the here and there well-known hymn, "If thou but suffer God to guide thee."

Since pastors are also teachers, consider teaching a course in hymns and con-gregational singing. The American Guild of Organists and the Hymn Society of America commissioned a study guide for such a course. Its title is *Hymns: a*

---

* *The Hymnody of the Christian Church,* p. 228.

Congregational Study, James Sydnor (Agape).

6. VARIOUS WAYS OF USING HYMNS

The usual way of singing hymns is to announce the hymn, have the organist play an introduction after which the congregation as a whole sings it straight through. There are other ways employed by many congregations which can give variety and fresh meaning to the singing. One of the simplest and most effective is described by Eric Thiman. After discussing descants and *faux bourdons* (melody in tenor) as a means of variety, he adds:

> It is strange that ministers and organists, knowing something of the method of singing the psalms employed in the temple at Jerusalem in pre-Christian times, do not make more use of the practice and possibilities of antiphonal singing.

He then states that this requires no elaborate preparation save to divide the congregation into sections such as folks on left and right of center aisle, balcony, transept, choir/congregation, women/men. The whole congregation sings the first and last stanzas. He continues:

> Few organists [and ministers] will have heard this done, and many will probably have no conception of how thrilling the "full" verses become when contrasted with the "sectional" ones.
>
> So simple is the idea that one can only marvel that it has not been tried to any extent; and as for the initial arrangements, it would only be necessary for the minister when announcing the hymn to indicate the allocation of verses; and in churches where a printed service paper is used, it could easily be printed thereon.
>
> There is that about antiphonal singing that seems to spur the congregation on to the best efforts possible; no doubt the natural feeling for emulation and competition is partly responsible; but there is in addition the fact that all parts of the congregation have a chance to rest their voices, with the result that when the turn of each section comes round, the allotted verse is attacked with freshness and enthusiasm. Be that as it may, the fact remains that where antiphonal singing has been tried, all are warmly in favour of it, and as a means of spurring on a lukewarm or lethargic congregation, there is no better method.*

Although any hymn can be sung antiphonally, certain hymns like "Watchman, tell us of the night" are a natural vehicle for this method of singing. The

* W. T. Whitley, *Congregational Hymn-Singing in England.* Quoted in *Music and Worship,* Davies and Grace, p. 144

* More challenging for small cong.

melodic structure of LASST UNS ERFREUEN "All creatures of our God and King" lends itself to antiphonal singing. The festival order of service in Chapter 10 includes many examples of dividing the congregation for antiphonal singing.

Recognize that hymns can be read as well as sung in public worship. Just because hymns are accompanied by music in hymnals does not mean that they must always be sung. A large number of hymns are prayers and could be incorporated in congregational prayers. You will be surprised at the additional insights you and your congregation gain by reading the texts.

Here are other modes of variation. The choir sopranos can sing, and instruments can play, a descant on a stanza. A varied harmonization, played occasionally by the organist, adds a festive note. Some hymn tunes lend themselves to canonic treatment. Chapter 6 gives a list of hymns which can be sung in canon. Addition of orchestral instruments can adorn the accompaniment. Bell choirs are widely used for hymn accompaniment. Newer hymnals are including notation for a variety of alternative accompaniments listed above.

It is apparent, of course, that all of these variations or alternate methods should not be employed in any one service. You will have to decide which procedure is appropriate for Sunday worship or for an occasion such as a hymn festival or hymn sing.

Chapter 5
THE ROLE OF MUSICIANS AND THE ORGAN

Playing hymns
Cantor/hymn leader
Training choirs for hymn leadership
Organ design and use

PLAYING HYMNS

The hymn player (at the organ, piano, or other instrument) can do more than any other one person to develop great hymn singing. No one else has as much control of the vital processes of hymn singing. The very life of the music flows through the spirit and fingertips.

1. *The hymn player is conductor of singing*

If there is no cantor standing in front of the congregation directing with gestures (and frequently there is not), the person playing the hymns is the conductor of the singing. The experienced congregational accompanist has discovered that he/she has much control over the singing of a group of people. The organist/pianist can indicate from the keyboard the mood and tempo of the music; can communicate the phrasing and some of the meaning of the text, and can fuse the random impulses of the group by a strong rhythmic leadership at the instrument.

Be sure to announce the hymn on your instrument at the tempo you want the people to sing and do not give a ritard at the end of this play-over. The player has learned to lead, not follow, the congregation. This does not mean racing helter-skelter toward the final chord with a few energetic members hanging on desperately. It does mean exercising control and using it with understanding. This sensitivity enables an instrumentalist to know how to vary touch from legato to some detachment or marcato which can nudge the people and bring them into line.

Part of conducting from the console (and especially introducing a new tune) is outlining the melody clearly. When the tune is brand new, some organists play melody only in octaves for one or two stanzas. Also the melody can be emphasized on a prominent reed stop. Use instruments, especially the trumpet, to double the melody with congregation.

2. *The hymn player is accurate.*

Accuracy is the foundation stone of music. Therefore hymn accompanists must strive constantly for complete accuracy, securing the hymn numbers before the service and diligently practicing the music until it is mastered.

There are two types of accuracy: (1) accuracy of pitch and (2) accuracy of time. The first of these is more readily achieved because it is the more obvious of the two types. Even the musically untutored member of the congregation winces at a discord. Accuracy of time value is more elusive but is absolutely essential because it affects the predictability and life of the music. It contributes to the rhythm and life pulse of the music. Many accompanists who shudder at a discord distort time values beyond recognition.

Here are three common errors in time values:
(1) *Failure to sustain long notes and to pull through dotted notes.* The habit of thinking of all long notes as being made up of several shorter notes tied together is most useful in developing sustained tone of proper length.

(2) *Tendency to shorten rests.* Hymn players should feel the pulse of the the music right through the silences.

(3) *Tendency to hurry eighth notes.* A British writer wrote, "The average singer [or pianist] tends to get too much pace on whenever the notes show tails."

Tune: ST. MARGARET

O   love   that wilt not let   me   go,

This person strives to maintain the rhythmic stride of the music. The player can find the remedy by "counting the time," by visualizing — or actually marking — the pulse beats above the score of each hymn. In Chapter 3 I marked some of the hymn scores with these pulse checkmarks. Frequent practice with a metronome, first slow, then progressively faster, will be an excellent aid in developing this accurate pulsation.

Fermatas This little symbol (⌒) is found in some hymnals at the end of phrases. Sometimes this means simply to catch a breath and move along. Other fermatas mean a pause. But the question is "How long?" In any event it should be an amount which will keep the basic overall pulsation intact. Fortunately many recent hymnal editors write in the exact time value of the interval between phrases.

Time signatures. Most musicians know how to interpret time signatures in hymns. However since there is considerable variation from hymnal to hymnal, we should give some explanation.

4/4. There are many stately tunes like EIN FESTE BURG "A mighty fortress" and DUNDEE "I to the hills will lift my eyes" in which the pulse occurs on each quarter note. But there are probably a larger number which require a faster pace. Here are examples. LANCASHIRE "Lead on, O King eternal" and HYMN TO JOY "Joyful, joyful, we adore thee" require a compelling forward stride which is better given if we feel an impulse on the first and third beats of each measure. ***In this case the 4/4 indication should be interpreted as 2/2.*** In other words, as a recent hymnal editor puts it, "In most hymns of duple meter, the half note represents the unit of pulse." Some hymnals use either 2/2 or $\downarrow$ to indicate the half note beat.

3/4. In certain triple time tunes, you feel the beat on each quarter note. BRIDEGROOM "As the bridegroom to his chosen" and WHITFIELD "We are your people" in Chapter 3 illustrate this pulsation. But brisker tunes like HYFRYDOL "Alleluia! sing to Jesus" and THREE KINGS OF ORIENT "We three kings of orient are" have a beat on the first note of each measure.

6/8. Almost without exception this time signature indicates two beats per measure. "Jesu, Jesu, fill us with your love" in Chapter 3 demonstrates this. Many of the Christmas carols have 6/8 time with a rollicking movement.

3/2. The half note is the unit of beat in melodies like KEDRON "Creating God, your fingers trace" displayed in Chapter 3.

No time signatures. An increasing number of hymnal editors are omitting many time signatures especially in early hymn tunes. How to you interpret this music? How do you find the pulse? How do you determine the pace? Suppose you are asked to play the following tune GAUDEAMUS PARITER.

When the King Shall Come Again

veal - ing, splen-dor shall an - nounce his reign,
a - tion; plants and flowers and sweet - est fruit
cheer - ful! God who comes for such as these
li - on, noth - ing e - vil or un -clean

life and joy and heal - ing; earth no long - er in de - cay,
join the cel - e - bra - tion; riv - ers spring up from the earth,
seeks and saves the fear - ful; now the deaf can hear the dumb
walks the road to Zi - on: ran - somed peo - ple home-ward bound

hope no more frus - trat - ed; this is God's re-
bar - ren lands a - dorn - ing; val - leys, this is
sing a - way their weep - ing; blind eyes see the
all your prais - es voic - ing, see your Lord with

demp-tion day long - ing - ly a - wait - ed.
your new birth, moun - tains, greet the morn - ing!
in - jured come walk - ing, run -ning, leap - ing.
glo - ry crowned, share in this re - joic - ing!

Text: Is. 35; Christopher Idle, b.1938, © 1982, Hope Publishing Co.
Tune: GAUDEAMUS PARITER, 7 6 7 6 D; Johann Horn, c.1495-1547

All you have to do is to read the text of Christopher Idle's Advent hymn to know that the tune must move with a lilt which matches the joy and hope of these words. Obviously the music must stride with the half note beat. To aid in keeping this pulse in mind, place check marks above the score to indicate this note value. Next, you will observe that the measures are irregular in length. Some have the equivalent of two half note beats and others have three. The first line, for example, has two measures of 2/2 and one measure of 3/2. So, rather than inserting a time signature to identify these distinctions, the editors simply left out the time signature.

When you get to the first measure in line four, you might be inclined to treat this as a 6/4 measure with two beats. But the correct interpretation is to continue the half note pulse and realize that this measure gives a delightful syncopation. Set your metronome at ♩ = 60 and see how it flows. A slow quarter note pulsation throughout this ancient tune would doom it to a slow death.

By the way, this tune frequently accompanies the Easter text "Come, you faithful, raise the strain." Editors of another contemporary hymnal have printed this Resurrection text and tune without any time signature *or bar lines.* Phrase endings are shown by an incise mark. For an example of unbarred music with no time signature, see NOW "Now the silence" in Chapter 3 which has incise marks to indicate phrase endings.

3. *The hymn player is rhythmical.*
Rhythm is more than a matter of time values. It is more than a steady succession of strong beats followed by one or more weak pulses. The word rhythm is derived from the Greek verb *rhein* meaning *to flow.* Rhythm therefore is synonymous with melodic and tonal movement. A competent organist/pianist does

LYONS

not play a beautiful melody in picket-fence fashion but rather flows through these chords and along the melody to certain points of climax and repose.

Hum or sing through each of the four phrases of LYONS "O worship the King" or "You servants of God" and observe climaxes marked by the asterisks. In the first, second, and last phrases, the point of emphasis is in the next to last measure. In the third phrase the climax is the last note. Played with these destinations in mind, your people will feel the rhythmic vitality in this fine tune.

4. *The hymn player uses a good tempo.*
The use of the correct tempo is probably the most important single aspect of good hymn playing. A common criticism of hymn accompaniment is that the instrumentalist dragged the tempo or played too fast. John Wesley in his "Directions for Singing" includes this caution: ". . .and take care not to sing too slow. This drawling way naturally steals on all who are lazy; and it is high time to drive it out from among us, and sing all our tunes just as quick as we did at first." Many of us organists/pianists are apt to err on the slow side.

However it is wise to have prejudice toward neither slow nor fast tempos but to judge each hymn by the internal nature of the music, by the emotion resident in the text, by the acoustics and by other factors. Just because some congregations tend to drag does not automatically call for rapid playing. The Editors of *Hymnbook 1982* (Episcopal) have placed a metronome indication below each hymn. Most of the metronome indications with the hymns in Chapter 3 were taken from this hymnbook. Keep a metronome on your piano or organ console and try out these tempi.

5. *The hymn player follows the text.*
A hymn player should pay attention to the text of all stanzas. Play the words as well as the music. Try to bring out the meaning of the text by careful phrasing. Note, for example, the final phrases of "How firm a foundation" (I'll never, no never, no never forsake) and "You servants of God" (Our Maker, Defender, Redeemer, and Friend).

As I play hymns I either sing quietly (in order to pay attention to how the congregation is getting along) or silently. In this way, I can empathize with the people's need for breathing.

VARIATION IN HYMN PLAYING

Abbreviated introductions
When a hymn is familiar, many organists shorten the introduction by playing

several sections (usually the first and last) which in connection make musical sense. This should identify the tune, give the pitch and pace, and allow enough time for the people to take the hymnal from the pew racks and find the place. Several hymnals have symbols above the score which identify how to abbreviate the music. Of course, if the hymn is new or somewhat unfamiliar, the entire piece should be played to help the congregation learn the tune.

Varied harmonizations

Different harmonies on certain stanzas adds interest to the playing and singing. This accompanimental device should not be overdone. Some organists are able to improvise this varied accompaniment. If you wish to begin the process of learning this skill, secure John Allen Ferguson's cassette with printed guide called *A Mini-Course in Creative Hymn Playing,* published by the American Guild of Organists, 475 Riverside Dr., Suite 1260, New York, NY 10015.

Several hymnals include alternative harmonizations with some hymns. Here are a few of the usual ones: LAUDES ANIMA "Praise, my soul, the king of heaven", AURELIA "The Church's one foundation", and WOODLANDS "Tell out my soul, the greatness of the Lord". A number of publishers have issued collections of alternate harmonizations for hymn tunes.

Hymn Intonations

A hymn intonation is an abbreviated instrumental introduction. Instead of playing the hymn (especially a familiar one) all the way through as printed in the hymnal, an organist can play a brief introduction which sets the mood of the hymn, shows the pace of the music, and outlines a part of the hymn melody. Several of the recent hymnals include hymns with these brief introductions. See, for example, "Ye who claim the faith of Jesus" in Chapter 3. Be sure to play intonations which are long enough to allow the congregation time to pick up their hymnal and find the place. Also I feel it is a mistake to play an intonation for a tune which is unfamiliar to a congregation. The people should hear the entire melody before trying to sing.

Other variations

Interest and variety can be added by certain accompanimental modifications. For example, in a hymn like "Christ the Lord is risen today" (LLANFAIR) in which each line ends with Alleluia, occasionally leave out the organ during the Alleluias on some stanzas. The people get a momentary exhilaration of unaccompanied singing. In some confident congregations, organists will leave out the organ during an entire stanza of some hymns.

Also, in a happy folk song like ROYAL OAK "All things bright and beautiful," play the refrain crisply. Certain stanzas can be accompanied by using
detached chords on the first and third beats of each measure after you have
gotten the folk started boldly.

An excellent practical guide for hymn players at the organ is Austin Lovelace's
The Organist and Hymn Playing. Revised Edition, (Agape, 1981).

HYMN PRELUDES.

Hymn tunes have been woven into much organ music for use as preludes,
voluntaries, and postludes. When these are played as part of worship, put a
note in bulletin saying where the hymn tune is located in the hymnal and
suggest that the congregation follow the prelude by reference to the hymn
score. It is helpful to preface the prelude by playing the hymn or chorale,
especially if the tune is not familiar and the prelude is highly ornamented.

Judy Hunnicutt has compiled an *Index of Hymn Tune Accompaniments for Organ,* published by the Hymn Society of America. Part One includes information about 191 collections of hymn preludes, free (varied) hymn accompaniments, introductions and/or interludes for organ. The contents of each collection are listed. Part Two provides an alphabetical listing of hymn tune names
with references to the collections in which the tune accompaniments are found.
And, of course, you can help the people learn a new hymn by playing it as a
prelude or interlude just as it is printed in the hymnal.

SIMPLIFIED ACCOMPANIMENTS

For beginning pianists and organists, there are collections of simplified hymn
accompaniments. I suggest *34 Easy Hymn Accompaniments for Organ* by Margaret Mealy, G.I.A. Publications, Inc. Here are several simplifications of tough
sections in two hymn tunes:

EASTER HYMN

Usual harmonization

Simpler version

HYFRYDOL
Usual harmonization

Simpler version

CANTOR/HYMN LEADER

A number of denominations are encouraging the use of cantors or song leaders in corporate worship as well as for informal gatherings. Although many congregations look to the keyboard for hymn leadership, it is frequently helpful to have a person directing the singing. As one pastor states: "The congregation appreciates an initial down beat as well as words being mouthed by the cantor, whether amplified or un-amplified." It is not necessary that the cantor be in front every Sunday or for every hymn or response. This person could be a choir member, the staff music director, or some other capable singer.* I have attended services where the hymn or service music leadership was shared by two persons.

It is not necessary that the cantor continue to beat the time throughout the hymn. Simply indicating with a gesture when to begin is frequently sufficient. The goal of this leadership is free intelligent spirited singing. The cantor is especially needed in responsorial singing of prose psalms and other liturgical refrains. The section on Service Music in Chapter 6 explains the responsorial method of singing.

TRAINING CHOIRS FOR HYMN LEADERSHIP

Choirs are committees of the congregation charged with responsibility for leadership of music in the service of worship. Although the singing of anthems and "special" music is important, the prime duty of choirs is the shepherding of the hymn singing. Of course, if the hymn is unfamiliar, the choirs should be taught it in rehearsal.

With the introduction of new hymns, ask the choir members to sing just the melody. It is unrealistic to expect the sopranos alone to outline the tune. The altos and men can assist in giving strong leadership by unison singing. This will be a large help to the people in the pews. And with familiar hymns, I ask my choir members to sing unison on the first and last stanzas. This gives a firm start and conclusion to the singing.

---

* *Hymns & Their Uses,* Sydnor (Agape) has a chapter on "The Conducting of Hymns."

And, as stated earlier, the choirs can sing new hymns as anthems and thus aid the people in the pews to learn the melody. Here are ways to adapt the various stanzas of hymns as anthems:

- All voices singing full harmony (accompanied or unaccompanied)
- All voices singing melody only
- Men singing melody alone
- Women singing melody alone
- Solo voice singing melody accompanied by choir humming the harmonies
- Altos, tenors, and basses singing melody with sopranos singing a descant
- A quartet, trio, or duet of solo voices
- A solo voice or section singing the melody with varied harmonization of accompaniment
- One or more stanzas sung in parts by women alone or men alone
- Modulation to a higher or lower key
- Changing from major to minor or reverse (e.g. ARFON, LLANGLOFFAN)

The Hymn Society of America publishes *A Listing of Currently Available Hymn Concertatos.* A hymn concertato is an extended hymn anthem.

Many churches use their children's choir to teach new hymns to the congregations. Mabel and Haskel Boyter taught new hymns to their congregation by means of the children's choir. Some of their methods are described in Chapter 8. The Choristers Guild, which is an international association of children's choir directors, publishes hymn study sheets and other aids for training the children in hymnody. The Guild's address is 2834 W. Kingsley Rd., Garland, TX 75401. Phone (214) 271-1521

ORGAN DESIGN AND USE

The pipe organ represents one of the great arts of the church; yet there is much confusion and ignorance in the mind of the church about this magnificent instrument. The scope of this book does not permit discussion of its design and use except to say that the tonal design and location of the instrument have a profound effect on the singing of the congregation. Resources now exist to guide local churches in the selection and purchase of an organ.

Here are titles to four guides which give ample and reliable information to assist churches in the process of securing an organ:

Ogasapian, John and Carlton T. Russell. *Buying an Organ.* American Guild of Organists, 475 Riverside Dr., Suite 1260, New York, NY 10015; $2.00. An eight page booklet commissioned by the Guild containing bibliography, brief discussion of topics, including how an organ works, buildings and acoustics, organ consultants, organ placement, costs, unification, electronic organs, etc. Offers a six step procedure for organizing and chairing an organ committee.

Fesperman, John. *Organ Planning: Asking the Right Questions.* The Church Hymnal Corporation, 800 Second Avenue, New York, NY 10017. $4.95.

Clemens, Philip K. *Choosing a Church Organ.* Mennonite Publishing House, Scottsdale, PA 15683. $0.50. A 10-page introduction to the organ selection process, zeroing in on the crucial matters.

Ogasapian, John. *Church Organs: A Guide to Selection and Purchase.* American Guild of Organists, 475 Riverside Dr., Suite 1260, New York, NY 10015. $6.95. A practical, easy-to-read, 135 page book dealing with various concerns of the organ committee.

The Royal Canadian College of Organists has established an Organ Resource Centre to provide churches with an objective and "disinterested" source of information. A comprehensive list of information available from this Centre can be obtained free of charge by writing: Organ Resource Centre, 515 McLeod Building, 10136-100 Street, Edmonton, Alberta, Canada, T5J OP1.

B. Educating the Congregation to Sing
Chapter 6
CONGREGATIONAL PRACTICES:
HYMNS AND SERVICE MUSIC

"For congregational singing to become the fine thing it may be, congregational practices are indispensable." I had never heard of the idea of rehearsing an entire church! Of course, I knew about practicing a choir but a congregational practice was a brand new notion. Sir Walford Davies continued:

> Only by such means can the faults that are inevitable in the first singing of an untrained mass be dispelled. Matters of simple discipline are contagious. For example, a congregation without great difficulty may be induced to start a hymn alertly and unanimously by a few minutes of practice.[1]

In Davies' chapter on "Congregational Singing" he went on to describe in detail how to plan and lead a hymn practice. Shortly after reading his explanation, I happened to read the Scottish *Manual of Church Praise* and found a similar chapter about congregation singing:

> Congregations through the land are willing and eager to learn. They are looking for guidance. If our organists will take up this subject seriously, and realize that it requires a technique of its own just as much as organ playing does, there is no reason why congregational singing, in even the smallest churches, should not become a worthy and acceptable offering.[2]

These descriptions made such good sense to me that I could hardly wait to try out the scheme. Since reading them, I have led congregational rehearsals in scores of different churches and conferences. The general response has been that people enthusiastically appreciate practical instruction in hymn singing and gain a new confidence and impetus in the service of praise.

WHAT ARE HYMN PRACTICES?

A hymn practice is an educational opportunity, carefully structured, for the congregation to learn how to sing hymns and service music with musicianship and intelligence and also how to broaden its repertory.

WHEN AND HOW LONG?

In one church where I was staff musician, I led a ten minute preservice hymn

---

1. Davies and Grace, *Music and Worship,* p. 145.
2. *Manual of Church Praise according to the Use of the Church of Scotland.* p. 157.

rehearsal once a month. In another church I led a hymn practice for about ② twenty minutes at each Wednesday evening fellowship supper. We would practice the hymns to be sung the next Sunday morning and give more general instruction. In some churches the practice takes the place of the announcement ③ ?! period within the service.

I have heard of some congregations where once in awhile the entire sermon ④ period is devoted to teaching methods of improving congregational praise. The vitality of future worship opportunities is thus measurably increased. In your particular situation, try to find a time when the entire congregation, or a large segment thereof, can be trained.

WHO LEADS?

The leader of these practices could be the music director (cantor), the minister, a chorister, or some other member of the church. Anyone with common sense, a gift of informal leadership, a singing voice, musicianship, and a love of hymns can do it. This person should stand in full view of the people and occasionally might rove up and down the aisles. The leader's voice is a better teaching medium than playing the tune on the organ. If there is a choir present, it could be asked to sit among the people and occasionally illustrate a snatch of melody. Sir Walford Davies suggests that "the less formal and schoolmasterish or ecclesiastical his method, the better." Remember that the people have assembled to sing hymns, not to listen to a lecture on hymnody or voice development. Enjoy yourself. Your enthusiasm will be contagious. Compliment and encourage the people. They can have fun on these occasions.

WHAT TO DO DURING THE REHEARSAL

Many leaders divide the time between working on hymns and on service music. Study the hymns beforehand so you know them perfectly. Plan every moment of the practice and write it down. Begin and end with a familiar hymn. Keep your comments and instruction succinct. Balance the learning of new hymns with giving fresh insights into familiar ones. Look up information about the hymns and share some with your people. Use chalkboard, overhead projector, or large easel if these will help your lesson plan.

Here are some specific projects on which the practice could focus:

① *Rehearse hymns for the following Sunday*
If there is an unfamiliar hymn scheduled, by all means teach it to the people and, preferably, work on it during several rehearsals before introducing it in the worship. Chapter 3 has help in teaching new hymns.

For the familiar hymns, give an explanation of some of the texts and their origin. Also call the people's attention to some interesting features of the music. Austin Lovelace's *Hymn Notes for Church Bulletins* (G.I.A. Publications) contains this background information in concise form. See Chapters 3 and 4 for samples of hymn backgrounds.

2. *Give general singing instructions*

In addition to teaching specific hymns, it is also profitable in each practice to give general principles which can guide your people in all their singing of hymns and service music. One of the best set of rules was given by John Wesley in a hymnbook printed in 1761. Called "Directions for Singing", these are printed at the end of this chapter in a form in which they can be photocopied and distributed to your congregation. Some leaders paste these on the flyleaf of each hymnal in the pews.

I have sometimes based a complete hymn practice on these Directions. After we read together a Direction, I gave further explanation of its meaning and then we sang one or more hymns in which we put that instruction into practice.

Here is a set of instructions by another Britisher, Plunket Greene:

a. "Never stop the march of a song." In other words, feel the pulse or beat of the tune and keep the hymn moving right to the end.

b. "Sing mentally through the rests." In congregational singing, this means that the people should listen to the playing over of the hymn by the piano or organ and thus get in the singing mood and pace. And if some other section is singing a particular stanza, pay attention to the text.

c. "Sing as you speak." That is to say, enunciate the words clearly and concentrate on the text.

Another general suggestion. Ask the people to make a habit of reading and reflecting on the hymns during the prelude. Then, to give focus to their attention, suggest that they always note to whom the hymn is addressed, and, as practice for this exercise, ask the people to look at the texts of the next Sunday hymns and say to whom the hymns are addressed. For example, "Joyful, joyful, we adore Thee" is addressed to God. In singing "Be still, my soul," we are speaking to ourselves. And in "Praise to the Lord, the Almighty," the worshippers are calling each other to offer praise and thanks to God.

Next, to increase the awareness of the meaning of texts, ask questions about certain obscure passages in hymns. For example, in "Guide me, O thou great Jehovah" there is the phrase "Death of death, and hell's destruction." Ask the people what this means.

3. *Employ lining out*

Illustrate how our ancestors used to learn and sing hymns. In remote churches where there were no books, hymns would be "lined out." Preachers or song leaders would speak or sing a line of a hymn and then lead the congregation in singing this line. The succeeding lines would be taught and sung in this way. The congregation probably knew from memory a few basic tunes in the familiar short, common, and long meters and could sing many texts to these few melodies. This lining out is a good way to teach a new hymn text and tune. Sing one line and let the people repeat it. Do the same with the other lines of the stanza. And we will see later in this chapter that lining out by cantors is an accepted mode of introducing refrains in public worship.

4. *Try various ways of singing*

Ask everyone to sing just the melody.

Request all who can sing harmony to do so, with the rest singing the tune.

Sing unaccompanied.

Change accompaniment. Use guitar or other instrument.

Have higher voices sing a descant.

Let the people sing a congregational stanza of a hymn anthem.

Have the people sing antiphonally with one side of the aisle singing first and the other side responding. "All creatures of our God and King" and "Watchman, tell us of the night" are well suited for this type of singing.

5. *Analyze hymn tune structure*

Take some time to explain the structure of hymn tunes. Not only will this interest the people but it also will assist them to analyze and master new hymn tunes. The structures of a number of tunes, familiar and new, are examined in Chapter 3.

Ch 3

6. *Explain page format*

Call the people's attention to the various editorial annotations on the hymnal page. Let them know that hymns are grouped according to categories listed in the Table of Contents and that the category of a particular hymn is printed on the hymn page. Show them where the details about author and composer are located. All of these items are explained in Chapter 2. Be sure to tell them that the tune is displayed in the top line of notes and ask them point to these notes while the music is sung or played.

Ch 2

7. *Show indexes and their uses*

Take the congregation on a walk through the indexes. Help them understand how hymns are selected for worship. Call their attention to the Topical Index. Point out the Tune Index. They may never have known that each hymn tune has a name. Explain how some have been named. Also you will find that they are especially interested in the Metrical Index which defines the metrical patterns. Give a simple brief explanation of this index and let the people experience swapping tunes. Ask them which tune they prefer for a given text. Chapter 2 gives information about Indexes.

8. *Sing alternate tunes*

Most hymnals have some hymns with two (sometimes three) tunes. When this occurs, it is frequently because one tune has been long used by the denomination but a new (sometimes better) musical setting has been found or created. Have the people sing both and let them express their opinions frankly as to which they prefer. Take time to teach them the less familiar one. The exchange of ideas will be helpful.

An illustration of this problem with alternate tunes is seen with the text "For all the saints." In the late nineteenth century this hymn was sung almost exclusively with the tune SARUM. In 1906 Ralph Vaughan Williams published the magnificent melody SINE NOMINE with this text and it gradually became the proper tune. Here are several other examples:

Jesus, lover of my soul MARTYN and ABERYSTWYTH
When I survey the wondrous cross HAMBURG and ROCKINGHAM OLD
Come, thou long expected Jesus HYFRYDOL and STUTTGART
All hail the power of Jesus' name CORONATION and MILES LANE

9. *Discuss hymn meanings with people*

Brian Wren suggests this method of helping a congregation concentrate on a text of a hymn:

1. After hearing the text read aloud, ask the congregation to read it in silence for three to four minutes (don't rush!). Each person can be invited to ask, for example: "Which lines make most impression on me? Why? Do I agree/disagree with what is said — why? What do I now want to do, or pray?" The hymn can then be sung by all.

2. Alternatively, before singing, ask people to share their thoughts with one or two immediate neighbors (beside them or behind — the latter may encourage contact with strangers if this is desirable). Allow three to four minutes for this sharing time, then all sing the hymn. Singing will be enriched because people have brought their own experience to the text.*

---

* *Praising a Mystery,* Hope Publishing Company, 1986. Used by permission.

10. *Sing canons and rounds*
The following tunes can be sung unaccompanied in canon at a distance of one measure. This can be a delightful and surprising experience. Be sure to have the entire group sing a stanza or so together before singing it in canon.

TALLIS CANON All praise to Thee, my God, this night
TOULON I greet Thee, who my sure Redeemer art
PURPOSE God is working his purpose out
ST. BRIDE Come, Lord, and tarry not
PUER NOBIS NASCITUR Unto us a child is born
DIX For the beauty of the earth
LONESOME VALLEY Jesus walked this lonesome valley
NEW BRITAIN Amazing grace, how sweet the sound
FOUNDATION How firm a foundation
RESIGNATION My shepherd will supply my need
HOLY MANNA God, who stretched the spangled heavens
ST. COLUMBA The king of love my shepherd is
MORNING SONG O holy city, seen of John (also "Lord, bid your ser-
                vant go in peace" which is a metrical version of
                Nunc Dimittis)
LAND OF REST Jerusalem, my happy home (also "I come with joy to
                meet my Lord")
SINE NOMINE For all the saints
RESTORATION Come, you sinners

The Hymnal 1982 (Episcopal) #710-715 includes rounds, such as "Dona nobis pacem," "Shalom, my friends," and "When Jesus wept." Here is a round based on the Angelic Song from *Worship,* 1986 (Roman Catholic), #401.

Gloria, Gloria

Glo - ri - a,   glo - ri - a,   in ex-cel - sis De - o!

Glo - ri - a,   glo - ri - a,   al - le -lu-ia,   al - le - lu - ia!

Text: Luke 2:14; Taizé Community, 1978
Tune: Jacques Berthier, b.1923
© 1979, Les Presses de Taizé

11.) Sing pentatonic hymn tunes

The pentatonic scale has five notes which can be heard by playing just the black keys on the piano. Tell your group that this scale is used throughout the world in folk music. At one congregational rehearsal I made a large chart of an octave of the piano keyboard which could be seen by the assembly and, as I sang "Amazing grace," I pointed to the black notes on my chart.

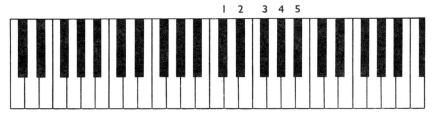

There are a number of the pentatonic hymn tunes in most hymnals, each of which some of your people could readily play on the piano. Just start on the particular black key which is numbered on the above chart.

PLEADING SAVIOUR Jesus, thou divine companion	5
˙ NEW BRITAIN Amazing grace	1
˙ FOUNDATION How firm a foundation	1
NOBODY KNOWS THE TROUBLE I'VE SEEN	5
RESTORATION Come, you sinners	2
HOLY MANNA God, who stretched the spangled heavens	1

12.) Teach some of the fundamentals of music reading

Recognize that some of your group may be excellent music readers but that many may not know one note from another. Put yourself in their places and don't be afraid to be elementary. Tell them that two components of a melody are pitch and length of note. Then give a brief explanation of each.

Musical pitches are arranged in series of tones called scales (derived from the Latin word for ladder or stairs). *La-la* a major scale for them or use numbers 1-8 and let your hand show the ascending and descending steps. Illustrate a descending scale by singing the first phrase of "Joy to the world." Find other hymns which clearly illustrate a complete or partial scale. The final phrase in DARWALL'S 148TH "Rejoice, the Lord is King" has an upward moving octave scale. ST. COLUMBA "The King of Love my Shepherd is" also illustrates the scale basis.

Then explain how some tunes skip up or down the scale. These are called a leaps. NICAEA "Holy, Holy, Holy, Lord God Almighty" employs leaps and steps.

Then, regarding rhythm, explain that hymn music is based on a steady succession of regular beats or pulses as if a group of people were marching. Some hymn tunes like HYMN TO JOY "Joyful, joyful, we adore Thee" have the large majority of its notes coinciding with the underlying regular beat. If you wish, point out that the quarter note (explain what one is) indicates this steady beat. But show that in several places Beethoven introduces eighth or dotted quarters for variety.

To show graphically what rhythmic variety means to the vitality of a hymn tune, let the people sing a fragment of "Silent night" using *only* a quarter note beat for every note of the melody. They will be so relieved when you let them restore the proper rhythm!

The extent and depth of your musical instruction will depend on your group, your ability, the amount of time and other factors. In any event, if your hymnal is the full harmony edition, ***show the people that the melody is in the top line of notes above the text.*** An extensive description of methods of teaching music reading to a congregation is included in Chapter 14 of *Hymns & Their Uses,* Sydnor (Agape).

PRACTICING SERVICE MUSIC

Service music is a broad term which generally means non-hymnic items which are sung by the congregation in the course of the public worship. This kind of music is usually brief. Ordinarily it does not have multiple stanzas. For these reasons it can be more easily memorized. Service music is most often prose although occasionally metrical. There is much diversity in these refrains and their musical settings. They are found in most denominational hymnals and also are listed in the catalogs of almost all publishers serving the liturgical market.

In churches with no prescribed liturgy these refrains are mainly the Ken Doxology, "Praise God from whom all blessings flow" and the Gloria Patri "Glory be to the Father". But in churches with an authorized liturgy there are many sung components in addition to hymns.

It is encouraging to note that in churches without a fixed liturgy there is an increasing movement toward the inclusion of a wide variety of musical expressions other than hymns, most of which are brief in scope. It should be emphasized that this music is to be sung by the congregation, not just by the choir. Of course, the choirs help the folk and it is desirable that during practice the choristers be often dispersed among the congregation. Proximity to a confident singer helps the amateur.

In hymnals the service music is either interprersed in the text of the liturgy or is located in a separate section of the hymnal. In some parishes, the sung responses are clearly printed in the service bulletin for ready reference by the congregation. And some denominations publish these refrains on cardboard sheets placed in the pew racks so that the people have ready access to this special music.

Types of service music

Here is a list of some of the types of service music:

— **The Ordinary.** Kyrie, Gloria, Credo, Sanctus, and Agnus Dei. In English translation, these have been woven in a variety of ways into the public worship of many denominations. These ancient texts have been set in plainsong, in the Merbecke version, in metrical form, and in other styles.

— **Acclamations.** These are opportunities for the people to break into praise expressing their faith. For example, before the reading of the Gospel or at some other place where jubilation is appropriate, the congregation can sing "Alleluia". In addition to the many special settings of Alleluia, some congregations excerpt just the Alleluias from a familiar hymn. Here are two examples:

O FILLII ET FILIAE "O sons and daughters, let us sing"

Al - le - lu - ia,   al - le - lu - ia,   al - le - lu - ia.

GELOBT SEI GOTT "Good Christians all, rejoice and sing"

Al - le - lu - ia,   al - le - lu - ia,   al - le - lu - ia.

Another acclamation is "Christ has died, Christ is risen, Christ will come again." At an appropriate moment in the liturgy, the leader says the following or some other invitation to praise: "Let us proclaim the mystery of our faith," Here is one setting of this text:

"Land of Rest"
Adapted by Richard Proulx, 1984
© GIA Publications

— *Responses to greetings by minister.*

— *Responses in litanies.*

— *Canticles.* Canticles are songs (other than Psalms) from the Bible. These are set in many musical forms for congregational use. Among them the following are most familiar.

A Song of Praise: "Benedictus es, Domine" Blessed art thou, O Lord God of our fathers
The Song of Mary: "Magnificat" My soul magnifies the Lord
The Song of Zachariah: "Benedictus Dominus Deus" Blessed be the Lord God of Israel
The Song of Simeon: "Nunc Dimittis" Lord, now lettest thou thy servant depart in peace
Glory be to God: "Gloria in excelsis" Glory be to God on high
We praise Thee: "Te Deum laudamus" We praise Thee, O God

— *The psalter*

Churches are now exploring many musical forms of expressing the psalter texts. Here are seven styles:

Psalm tone	Cantillation	Taizé (ostinato)
Gregorian psalm tone	Metrical psalm	
Anglican chant	Gelineau	

Here are examples of two methods of singing psalms, canticles, and responses:

Gelineau. In the Gelineau responsorial psalms, a leader sings the verses and the assembly responds with an antiphon. In the setting of Psalm 23, Joseph Gelineau provided three antiphons, the first of which follows:

Joseph Gelineau, 1963
© GIA Publications

Taizé. The music from the French ecumenical community of Taizé is a further development of the refrain approach which can be used with psalms, canticles, and other responses. In this case, however, the refrain is commonly repeated over and over as an ostinato, with other parts (solo verses and instrumental solos) superimposed. G.I.A. Publications has issued two volumes of *Music from Taizé* with instructions as to the use of this music. Also available from this publisher are several recordings of live performances of assemblies singing Taizé music. On the next page there is an example of *Music from Taizé*

After the ostinato is established, the choir may gradually add the choral harmonies in the specified order. A vocal soloist can sing verses over the ostinato, or an instrument can play melody lines, found in a separate book of instrumental parts. A flute part is included here. This particular piece could be very effective for confirmation or ordination, or as a prelude to the liturgy. The flexibility of the verses and ostinato allow the Taizé music to be tailored to the exact amount of time or music needed.

Veni Sancte Spiritus

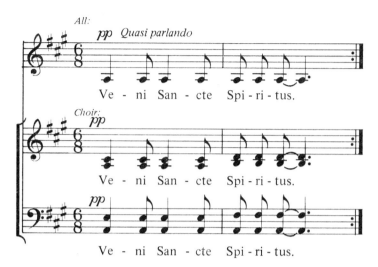

Verses

As the ostinato continues, vocal and instrumental verses are sung or played as desired with some space always left between the verses (after the cantor's "Veni Sancte Spiritus").

Text: *Come Holy Spirit;* Verses drawn from the Pentecost Sequence; Taizé Community, 1978
Tune: Jacques Berthier, b. 1923
© 1979, Les Presses de Taizé

Most refrains are sung in two ways. In one way, the cantor sings the refrain
and the people repeat it as shown in the following Acclamation. The advantage
of this routine is that the assembly hears the tune modeled just before they are
to sing it. For example:

Frank Schoen, 1970
© GIA Publications

Another setting follows, this one being a complete setting of Eucharistic acclamations.

Then there are pieces which the people sing by themselves without preliminary
prompting. The instrumentalist plays a measure or so of introduction so the
people can hear the tempo, the key and an intimation of the melody. Then they
sing.

There are many ways of teaching these refrains. Sir Walford Davies says, "The
best teaching medium is the conductor's voice, so the first desideratum in the
conductor is a voice which he is neither afraid nor unable to raise (more or less
pleasantly) in song as well as in speech."[1] After its singing by the cantor and/or
choirs, the entire congregation can sing it. Be sure to repeat each refrain until it
becomes engrained in the corporate memory. These congregational refrains
should preferably be sung from memory in the service.

---

1. *Music and Worship.* p. 146.

Eucharistic Acclamations

Choir harmony for all or some refrains

Ho - san - na! Ho - san - na! Ho - san - na in the high - est!

(+ Assembly)

Ho - san - na! Ho - san - na! Ho - san - na in the high - est!

Ho - san - na! Ho-san - na in the high - est!

Ho - san - na! Ho-san - na in the high - est!

"Mass of the Divine Word"
Howard Hughes, SM, 1981
© GIA Publications

Easy steps toward congregational participation in responsorial psalm singing. This skillfully graded method of teaching psalm singing was developed by Hal Hopson.[2]

Step 1. A reader and the congregation read the verses responsively with the choir interjecting a refrain after each pair of verses. The refrain should be a phrase from a well-known hymn. This first step gets the congregation accustomed to having a refrain as a part of the psalmody in the service.

(from "For the beauty of the earth")

Refrain

Lord of all, to Thee we raise This our hymn of grate-ful praise.

Psalm 100:1-4

1. All the lands make joy to you, O God;

2. WE SERVE YOU WITH GLADNESS; WE COME INTO YOUR PRESENCE WITH SINGING:

REFRAIN

3. You are the Lord our God; You made us, and we are yours; We are your people, and the sheep of your pasture.

4. WE ENTER YOUR GATES WITH THANKSGIVING, AND YOUR COURTS WITH PRAISE; WE GIVE THANKS TO YOU, WE BLESS YOUR NAME.

REFRAIN

Step 2. A reader and the choir read the verses responsively with the choir and congregation singing the refrain after each pair of verses. Again, the refrain should be a phrase from a well-known hymn.

---

2. Copyright 1984 Hal H. Hopson. Used by permission.

Step 3. A reader and the congregation read the verses responsively with the choir and congregation singing an antiphonal refrain.

Refrain

Step 4. A reader and the congregation read the verses responsively with the choir singing the refrain. (See ***A below***)

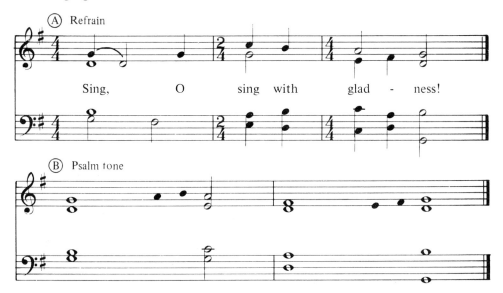

Step 5. A reader reads the verses. The choir and congregation sing a specially composed refrain like refrain ***A*** above.

Step 6. Cantor chants the verses on a simple tone (see ***B*** above) with the choir and congregation singing the refrain (see ***A*** above)

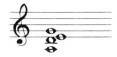

Optional handbell, or this cluster chord.

Mode of display of responsorial psalmody.

A common method of displaying a psalm and refrain(s) in a hymnal is to have one or more responses printed at the head of the page. One of these may be a fragment of a familiar hymn. For example, "Sing praise to God who reigns above" MIT FREUDEN ZART or "A mighty fortress is our God" EIN FESTE BURG. Underneath is the psalm divided into the verses or sections to be read or sung by the leader and assembly. The people's part is frequently indented and set in bold face or capitals. The bold initial **R,** meaning Refrain, is located before and after the psalm as well at one or more appropriate points in the psalm. Elsewhere there is usually a page of instructions giving a set of simple psalm tones to which the leader's part may be sung.

The wide variety of methods of reading/singing a psalm is shown in the following typical instructions:

1. The leader reads the light type and the group reads the boldface type, or the light and boldface type may be read alternately by two groups, such as the right and left sections of the congregation, or other voice groupings; or the psalms may be read in unison.

2. Following traditional patterns, responses are included at the beginning of each psalms for emphasis and illumination. These hymn and scripture responses are spoken or sung at the beginning and end of each psalm and at the places designated by **R.**

3. The method for reading the psalms and singing the responses:

    A.   A solo voice or choir sings the response, followed by the congregation singing the response.

    B.   A leader or group begins reading the light text of the psalm in alternation with the congregation as in #1 above.

    C.   The congregation sings the response where it is indicated by **R** and at the conclusion of the psalm.

4. This same pattern is followed when the responses are read.

DIRECTIONS FOR CONGREGATIONAL SINGING
John Wesley

Sing all. See that you join with the congregation as frequently as you can. Let not a slight degree of weakness or weariness hinder you. If it is a cross to you, take it up, and you will find it a blessing.

Sing lustily, and with a good courage. Beware of singing as if you are half-dead or half-asleep; but lift up your voice with strength. Be no more afraid of your voice now, nor more ashamed of its being heard, than when you sing the songs of Satan.

Sing modestly. Do not bawl, so as to be heard above or distinct from the rest of the congregation — that you may not destroy the harmony — but strive to unite your voices together so as to make one clear melodious sound.

Sing in time. Whatever time is sung, be sure to keep with it. Do not run before nor stay behind it but attend close to the leading voices, and move therewith as exactly as you can; and take care not to sing too slow. This drawling way naturally steals on all who are lazy; and it is high time to drive it out from among us, and sing all our tunes just as quick as we did at first.

Above all, sing spiritually. Have an eye to God in every word you sing. Aim at pleasing him more than yourself, or any other creature. In order to do this, attend strictly to the sense of what you sing, and see that your heart is not carried away with the sound, but offered to God continually; so shall your singing be such as the Lord will approve of here, and reward you when he cometh in the clouds of heaven.

Chapter 7
HYMNS IN HOMES

Hymns are for homes as much as for churches. And yet, I fear, most churchgoers experience hymns only in church. Of course, there are some folk who know hymns by heart and hum or sing them as they go about washing dishes or cleaning the house. But, for many others, the singing on Sunday morning is their sole encounter with hymns.

In England it is different. On Sunday night upwards of 10 million are watching and joining in a British Broadcasting Company program called "Songs of Praise." From midsummer until Easter, it's the prime time front runner among Britain's Sunday evening television programs. It promotes no cause and preaches no message, except the message that Christians love to sing their faith. Each week, a different site is chosen for the broadcast — usually a church or college chapel, although an occasional special is done outdoors. In one grand, nationwide, weekly hymn sing, people all over the British Isles do exactly that. It's naturally ecumenical, low-keyed and pure joy — and it's in their homes!

When is the last time you took any measures to get hymnals and hymn singing back into the home? Two sixteenth century church leaders, John Calvin and Martin Luther, did this and created a people devoted to singing their faith.

On my study shelves is a facsimile of the first Genevan psalter dated 1542. Its size is 4 by 6 inches and a half inch thick. In it are metrical psalms with a melody line. This book of praise and prayer was not kept in the pews of the church but in the homes. Before leaving for church, they stuck the psalter in their pocket. A visitor to John Calvin's church in 1557 wrote this note in his diary: "There each one draws from his pocket a small book which contains the psalms with notes, and out of full hearts, in the native speech, the congregation sings before and after the sermon. Every one testifies to me how great consolation and edification is derived from this custom."

Luther, likewise, published pocket sized hymnals with text and tunes. One writer, speaking of Luther, said that he took hymns out of the liturgies and put them into people's hearts and homes, that when they had learned them and loved them, they might bring them to the church and sing them together.

When I was a lad, I observed this custom repeated. Two maiden ladies in my father's congregation had the pew just in front of ours. I frequently watched them open their purses and take out little books of *Psalms and Hymns*. Years later one of them, Miss Mary Hopkins, gave me her well-worn copy. It is 5 by

3 inches. Hymn after hymn has marginal notes showing they had been read and pondered.

A most rewarding task of church leaders is to use every possible means to get the hymnal and hymns back into the homes of our members. We will talk first about how hymns can be used in homes and, then, we will suggest some ways for getting them into homes.

USES OF HYMNS IN HOMES

Early childhood and hymns

When Sabine and Dietrich Bonhoeffer were six weeks old, two Moravian ladies from the Community of Brethren at Herrnhut were engaged to look after the children in the privileged Bonhoeffer home in Breslau. The father was head of a psychiatric clinic and a prominent physician. Fräulein Käte was in charge of Sabine and Dietrich. Dietrich later became the famous theologian. Sabine Leibholz, twin sister of Dietrich, described their early love of hymns. She wrote:

> [Käte] gave us at home our first year's teaching. Dietrich loved her devotedly and eagerly made himself into a helpful Brownie for her . . . Among the songs which Dietrich especially loved were: 'Where the Soul Finds Its Home, Its Rest,' 'Wait, My Soul,' 'Jesus, Guide Our Way,' 'Now let us go and Make Our Way with Singing and with Praying.' He called these hymns 'red songs.' We also had 'black songs;' 'Praise Ye the Lord' and 'Now Thank We all Our God,' for example, were 'black songs.' The *red* and *black* were part of a speech code kept secret between us two. For the evening singing we were allowed to choose the hymns, but if we hesitated too long, our mother made the choice herself. She knew all the verses of most of the hymns by heart. After the light was put out, our illuminated crucifixes, glowing with phosphorus, were our joy. The light was comforting but often the shape of the cross troubled us.*

When our daughters were infants, we tucked them in bed with a prayer, a hymn, and a kiss. From their earliest days, they heard stanzas from such hymns as "If thou but suffer God to guide thee", "O God, our help in ages past," and "Now the day is over." And, of course, they were taught "Jesus loves me." When Karl Barth, the eminent Swiss theologian, was asked to sum up his theology, he is reported to have said, "Jesus loves me, this I know."

---

* *Union Seminary Quarterly Review.* Vol. XX, No. 4. May 1965. Article "Dietrich Bonhoeffer: A Glimpse into our Childhood." (Copyright 1965 by Union Theological Seminary in the City of New York. Used by permission.)

Grace at mealtime

Martin Rinkart, pastor in the walled city of Eilenburg during the Thirty Years War (1618-1648), wrote "Now that we all our God" as a *tischgebet* — a grace to be sung at table by his family. This expression of courage and good cheer is remarkable, coming from the midst of the calamities of war.

Many families sing a hymn stanza or just a line as a blessing. We sing sometimes either the first line or the entire first stanza of "Now thank we all our God." Other times we sing the round "For rest and food and loving care." The familiar grace "God is great and God is good, and we thank him for this food" fits a number of hymn tunes which have the 7.7 meter. For example, try this grace to the tune of the refrain of "For the beauty of the earth" which is "Lord of all, to thee we raise this our hymn of grateful praise." The Bishop Ken Doxology and many other hymn stanzas or fragments can be sung as a blessings.

Hymns in daily devotions

On July 17, 1722, a little group of Christian refugees came to the estate of Count Nicolaus Ludwig von Zinzendorf in Saxony, Germany. They were spiritual and lineal descendants of the sturdy founders of the ancient *Unitas Fratrum,* established March 1, 1457. To encourage these Moravians, the Count would select a Scripture passage or two and a hymn stanza and announce them each day to these Christians. The Moravians maintain this custom to the present time.

There are varieties of ways Christians use hymns for spiritual sustenance. In the manse where I was raised, we had family prayers each morning. In addition to Bible reading and prayers, we sang a hymn. I know a couple who have their daily prayers at the breakfast table and always include reading a hymn. And, of course, hymns can become a part of private daily prayers. A majority of the hymns are prayers addressed to the triune God and can serve in increasing the vocabulary and meaning of prayer.

One day years ago I visited Miss Bellamy who was an aged invalid confined to the upstairs of her spacious home. Hearing that I was teaching a class in hymnody at her church, she said, "Sometimes when I am in my room alone at night, I feel lonesome. But I begin repeating hymns I know from memory, starting at the beginning of the alphabet. 'A mighty fortress,' 'Abide with me,' and so on. Before long, I drop off to sleep contented."

Family hymn sings

Robert Burns describes a Scottish family's singing metrical psalms in his poem

"The Cotter's Saturday Night." The father reads scripture and then, writes Burns,

> They chant their artless notes in simple guise:
> They tune their hearts, by far the noblest aim;
> Perhaps "Dundee's" wild warbling measures rise,
> Or plaintive "Martyrs," worthy of the name;
> Or noble "Elgin" beets [feeds] the heavenward flame,
> The sweetest far of Scotia's holy lays.

Burns comments on this scene by saying, "From scenes like these old Scotia's grandeur springs." Several of these psalm tunes are still found in our contemporary hymnals.

Dietrich Bonhoeffer's family had a lovely Christmas eve custom of reading the Christmas story, singing carols, and lighting the tree candles. Decades later Bonhoeffer wrote; "A Christian family fellowship will try to master as large as possible a number of hymns that can be sung freely from memory."[1]

The Luthers sang hymns in their home in Wittenberg. One very special occasion was a Christmas Eve family celebration about 1534. Luther had written a fourteen stanza hymn based on a popular carol of the day. It was "From heaven above to earth I come" set to the tune VOM HIMMEL HOCH. The first few stanzas were sung by a neighbor dressed as an angel, heralding the birth of Christ, and the next several stanzas were sung by the children in response to the angel's message, with all the family joining in the last stanza. Some hymnals are now including all fourteen stanzas.[2] Incidentally this hymn and its origin makes an excellent scenario for a Christmas play or pageant. Try writing one.

One Christmas eve our family had a three hour open house, a major feature of which was carol singing. Six pianist friends were scheduled on half hour stints to accompany those who cared to move from the punch bowl and conversation to the piano where small carol booklets were available.

Once during a weekend hymnody workshop in a large urban church, the governing body and music committee (about seventy people in all) were invited to a buffet supper in a spacious home. After supper we gathered for a very informal and delightful singing of familiar and new hymns using the church hymnal.

---

1. *Life Together* by Dietrich Bonhoeffer (translated by J. W. Doberstein), p. 81. Copyright 1954 by Harper and Row. Used by permission.
2. The complete carol can be found in *Worship* No. 388 (G.I.A. Publications) and *Lutheran Book of Worship*, No. 51.

Learning hymn playing

If there is a piano in the home, a hymnal on the rack will encourage hymn playiɪg. Also when the children are taking piano lessons, suggest that the teacher include hymn playing in the tuition. Purchase a copy of *34 Easy Hymn Accompaniments* by Margaret Mealy (G.I.A. Publications, Inc.) for the beginners.

GETTING HYMNS AND HYMNALS INTO HOMES

As you plan ways to restore the use of hymns in homes, keep in mind that many of your members probably have never thought of the idea. They need to know how other folk utilize hymns for private and family use and they require help in ways to go about it.

1. The most obvious way is to urge families to purchase a hymnal. In fact, if a congregation is acquiring new hymnals, suggest that their members buy two copies — one for use in church and one for the home.

2. Since some people may feel that they cannot afford a hymnal, consider compiling a small collection of hymns printed on the church's copying machine or elsewhere. There are hundreds of excellent hymns which are in public domain whose texts can be made available for home use. License to use copyright material can be obtained from publishers.

3. Leaders can help organize home hymn sings. Ask people with sufficient space to open their homes for an evening of hymn singing. It is not necessary always to have a piano for accompaniment, though this is helpful. Offer to supply leadership and hymnals. Pot luck refreshments might be provided. Tell the folk that the hymn sing will last a specific amount of time, perhaps two hours (say, seven to nine o'clock). Bring children. Mention that this will be an all-request sing. It is not necessary to sing all stanzas of each hymn. If the leader knows some background of hymns, let a brief comment be made but avoid lecturing. Have a good time.

4. Occasionally print the texts of one or more of the hymns for the following Sunday in the bulletin and suggest that the people read it/them in devotions during the following week. You would almost certainly observe an increased and more intelligent hymn singing the next Sunday.

Chapter 8
HYMNS AND EDUCATION

"It is the hymns, repeated over and over again, which form the container of much of our faith. They are probably in our age the only confessional documents which we learn by heart. As such, they have taken the place of our catechisms . . . There is ample literature about the great formative influence of the hymns of a tradition on its members. Tell me what you sing, and I'll tell you who you are!"[1] These words by Albert van den Heuvel of the World Council of Churches underscore the didactic power of hymns.

A recent writer reiterates this thought. "Hymns still do much of the teaching that goes on among Christians. I would guess that you can remember a lot more hymn lines than Bible verses; and when you don't know what to pray, you are likely to fall back on the words of a hymn."

Each chapter of *Introducing a New Hymnal* has been devoted to the education of church people in the fullest possible use of hymns but this chapter deals specifically and briefly with the part which hymns play in the teaching enterprises of a congregation. Although Christian education occurs in many activities of a congregation (public worship, fellowship suppers, small Bible study groups, etc.), we usually think of it specifically in relation to the church school. Classes in hymnody may be held during the week but especially on Sunday. Also we should not forget that a major opportunity for learning about hymns are in the rehearsals of the choir(s).

HYMNS FOR CHILDREN

A recent denominational hymnal includes a preface to its Index of Hymns for Use with Children which begins:

Hymnody is perhaps more important to very young Christians than it is to the mature members of the congregation. Hymns help to incorporate children into the worshiping community. By joining in the singing children can experience a fullness of participation difficult for them to feel in some other parts of the liturgy. Hymns tell the story of the faith, provide vehicles for the liberation of soul and spirit, and teach theology and church history. They can both educate and form young Christians.[2]

---

1. *Risk: New Hymns for a New Day.* Preface. Copyright 1966 by World Council of Churches. Used by permission

2. *Hymnbook* 1982.. Episcopal. Copyright 1985 by The Church Pension Fund.

If your hymnal does not have an index which singles out hymns suited especially to childhood, assign a small task force to list those hymns which are appropriate to the young mind and spirit. In fact, this assignment could be a part of a larger project, namely to compile a graded hymnic curriculum for the entire church school, one which is based on the denominational hymnal. This list could be the basis for instruction of persons as they pass along through the educational system of a congregation.[1]

It is well nigh fatal to hold one standard in the more formal church worship and then "let the bars down" in the church school. Having one type of Sunday school hymns and then expecting the children to enjoy and appreciate the hymns announced in church worship is an exercise in futility. We will again be training a generation of Christians who will always find worship somewhat frustrating. Their complaint will be that of many of their parents, "Why can't we sing something we know?"

A unique intergenerational approach to learning hymns was employed by Mabel and Haskell Boyter of Atlanta, Georgia. They attacked the problem from the 7-year old children up through the youth choirs. In choir rehearsals, twenty-five new hymns were taught the children during the season (October to June). In addition to this group work, a hymn memorizing contest was announced. It would extend from October 15 to May 15. The rules were as follows:

Each child was to
  a. memorize the melody,
  b. memorize the first stanza, and
  c. sing melody and first stanza from memory unaccompanied before the "listening committee."

Adequate records were kept and tabulated by a Hymn Chairperson with monthly announcements of who was ahead in the contest. Such remarkable response was received that the listening committee had to be doubled within eight weeks' time.

The important feature regarding this project was the fact that these hymns were *selected and taught by the parents of the choristers.* This was the first wedge in a *family* project. Later, when enthusiasm was rampant, a "Family Hymn Sing" was announced, with recognition to be given the 100 percent families who were present. There were 23 families who were 100 percent present! Be-

---

1. Two such lists can be studied in *The Hymn and Congregational Singing.* James Sydnor (John Knox Press) and *Sing with Understanding,* Harry Eskew and Hugh T. McElrath. (Broadman Press)

tween 250 and 300 people attended and sang more enthusiastically than most of the Sunday morning congregations. The Hymn Sing was held Sunday afternoon between 3:30 and 4:30 o'clock. The fact that this "Sing" was announced as lasting exactly one hour played a large part in its success. All the promotional communications stated that even if the congregation was in the middle of a hymn, they could count on exactly one hour for this project. Besides improving congregational singing, it was hoped that through this "family affair" the old custom of family singing in the homes could be revived, at least to a certain extent.

A second "Sing" was held a month later with almost 400 people present and 27 families were 100 percent there. A revealing fact was *the exposure to 19 new hymns* besides many old or familiar hymns which were sung during the two one-hour sessions. The boys and girls who already knew these new hymns were urged to *hold hymnals with their fathers and mothers* and thus to lead them in the learning of new materials. At the same time a feeling of family togetherness was felt more and more strongly.

****

Space does not permit detailed instruction about teaching hymns to children. The following books will give this aid:

Our Heritage of Hymns — Leader's Guide by Mary Nelson Keithahn. A program for teaching hymns to children. The guide contains study sheets, background on the hymns, and methods of teaching. A cassette recording is also available. Secure through the Hymn Society Book Service.

Music in Church Education with Children by Helen Kemp, published by Choristers Guild.

HYMNS IN CHURCH SCHOOL CLASSES

The education committee should give careful consideration as to the use of hymns in the learning process. Remember that youth and adult singers are able to help teachers who need assistance. Denominational lesson plans for church school classes sometimes incorporate hymns in the material. If the lesson deals with a Bible passage, consult the Index of Scriptural Allusions in your hymnal to find other hymns which are commentaries on the particular passage. Some hymns are based very closely on Scripture, such as the metrical psalms and hymns like "How firm a foundation" which is essentially an entire quotation from the Old Testament. Jacob's experience at Bethel is the basis for these hymns: "O God of Bethel, by whose hand" and "Nearer, my God, to Thee."

If the lesson deals with a theological topic, you may find reference to an illuminating hymn in the Topical Index. For example, there are a number of excellent hymns based on the doctrine of the Trinity. Hymns like "O sing a song of Bethlehem" and "Hope of the world, thou Christ of great compassion" summarize the entire life and ministry of Jesus.

Charles Wesley's many hymns describe the myriad aspects of Christian experience. A class in church history can be admirably illustrated by hymns from the various periods.

It would be entirely appropriate to include in the youth and adult curriculum a class devoted exclusively to hymnody. The Hymn Society of America and the American Guild of Organists commissioned a text for such a class — *Hymns: a Congregational Study,* Sydnor (Agape).

Many people agree that church schools should provide opportunity, preferably each Sunday, for the entire student body to assemble for a brief period of hymn singing as a group. Granted they can sing hymns in church worship, it is helpful to sing in this less formal atmosphere.

Each church educational system is unique in some respects. Therefore study it and devise a hymn curriculum that suits the needs of your children and adults. The rewards will be limitless.

Chapter 9
ACOUSTICS AND HYMN SINGING

Would you line the interior of your Stradivarius violin with a thick felt pad? Certainly not. The sound waves from the strings need to be selectively modified and amplified by the exquisitely shaped cavity so that the tones which reach the ears of the listeners are beautiful.

And yet this preposterous proposal is analogous to what we do with our worship spaces. The former president of The Hymn Society of America, Robert Batastini, wrote:

> The problem which especially concerns me is the acoustical environment for congregational singing. It seems as though it is now the clear norm for new and renovated worship spaces to be carpeted. Pew cushions are another common furniture item. The effect of these materials on the song of the assembly is devastating. What carpeting does to the ability of one congregant to hear the voice of another, or more importantly of the whole, seriously diminishes the joyful noise of the singing assembly.[1]

Paul Westermeyer, Editor of The Hymn, echoes this concern. He wrote:

> Recently I returned from a tour with my college choir. Every church we sang in was carpeted. The newest church, built very recently, had thick padding on the floor, cushions on the backs and seats of the pews, and framed squares of carpeting on brick walls which appeared to be treated to absorb sound. We sing in churches of many denominations. I visit churches of many denominations as well as synagogues and temples, both in connection with my teaching and on my own. Each year carpeting and absorbent materials seem to increase everywhere.[2]

Another testimony to the importance of correct church acoustics pertains also to economics. Joseph Blanton wrote:

> The current extensive and indiscriminate use of sound-absorbing materials in churches is one of the most deplorable developments in contemporary church practice. It is a common experience today for a church group to spend several thousand dollars for sound-absorbing materials which render the interior of their new church acoustically dead. This in turn calls for

---

1. *The Hymn: A Journal of Congregational Song.* July, 1987. p. 6. Published by The Hymn Society of America.

2. *The Hymn: A Journal of Congregational Song.* July, 1987. p. 5. Published by The Hymn Society of America.

the spending of hundreds of dollars more for an amplifying system to enable the congregation to hear the preacher and many more thousands of dollars for additional ranks of pipes for the organ which would be wholly unnecessary if they had not spent the money for the acoustical materials in the first place. This is a vicious sequence of expenditures which ends up with the church having put out a lot of extra money for an inferior result; in some cases of very large projects these ill-advised expenditures reach prodigious sums.[1]

My experience has been the same. With my choir on tour, I have stood in the chancel of some church and heard the complete tonal spectrum of the organ and choir, but as I walked down the aisle, the tone progressively deteriorated. What had happened was that the beautiful initial tones were being swallowed up in the millions of traps in the cinder block walls of the chancel and auditorium, or in the myriad recesses of pew cushions, or in the deep piling of the carpets, or in the 2,349,871 holes in the ceiling blocks!

And I am not concerned here primarily with the sounds of speaking voice, choir, or organ (although these are important) but with the effect which bad acoustics has on the persons in the pews who are trying to sing hymns. Referring to congregational singing, Sir James Jeans, eminent British physicist, said that a non-reverberant room "produces the despair of ineffectual struggle" whereas, he continues, sufficient reverberation "naturally induces an exhilarating feeling of effortless power."[2]

Sir James speaks of reverberation. What does he mean by "sufficient reverberation"? Scott R. Riedel explains it this way:

> The reverberation period is the single most important factor in developing a desirable acoustical condition in a worship space. The proper reverberation period will encourage vigorous congregational singing and spoken response. It will lend grace and beauty to organ, choral, and instrumental music. Musicians will find tuning and rhythm to be more precise in a desirable reverberative setting. The spoken word gains volume and authority in a properly reverberative setting. A reverberation period that is too short will leave music dull and lifeless and without tuning stability, and speech will seem distant and weak. A reverberation period that is too long will render music and speech confused and unintelligible. The cor-

---

1. *The Organ in Church Design.* p. 111. Albany, Texas: Venture Press, 1957. (Copyright 1957 by Joseph E. Blanton. Used by permission).

2. *Science & Music.* p. 212. Cambridge: Cambridge University Press, 1937.

rect reverberation period is essential to the success of vigorous worship.

The reverberation period is the number of seconds that sound will linger in a given space. Specifically, it is the amount of time in seconds that sound energy will take to drop 60 decibels after the source has ceased producing a tone. The function and use of a space determines its appropriate reverberation period. In rooms to be used for liturgical worship, where speech, corporate spoken response, corporate singing, and liturgical choral and organ music are the primary sound sources, a reverberation period near two seconds at mid-range frequencies is desirable.*

What happens specifically when sound vibrations leave the throats of the congregation? These sound waves pass through the air until they hit a surface. Here they are either reflected to some other surface or they are absorbed. Everyone has seen the little holes in acoustical blocks. The vibrations pass through these holes and are trapped. Most of the sound does not emerge. The same thing happens when vibrations hit clothing, draperies, pew cushions, and non-acoustical carpeting.

In public dining rooms, in halls of school buildings, in living rooms at home, and in all places where noise is generated and little sound is wanted, these are places where sound damping is indicated. If a person wants to enjoy singing at home, he/she does not stand in a clothes closet and sing. The bathroom with its hard reflective surfaces is the best place.

In planning a new church sanctuary, be sure to engage an architect who has a track record of planning acoustically excellent church interiors. This person will consider both the needs of the spoken word of the minister as well as the voices of the congregation. If the present worship room has inferior acoustics, keep in mind that corrective measures are possible. The acoustical blocks can be painted over to obliterate the absorption pores. The carpets can be replaced with hard tile or other reflective flooring.

The interior of a church is an instrument — an instrument of God — and it should be so formed that the spoken word can be heard by all worshipers and the praise, whether vocal or instrumental, is beautiful and full of meaning.

---

* *Acoustics in the Worship Space,* Scott R. Riedel. Church Music Pamphlet Series, Carl Schalk, Editor. Copyright 1986 by Concordia Publishing House. Used by permission. This booklet is packed with good acoustical information and helpful bibliography.

Chapter 10
HYMN FESTIVALS/HYMN SINGS

The terms — hymn festivals, hymn sings, and hymn practices — as used in this book, have different meanings. A hymn festival is a celebration of the Christian faith with the singing of hymns based on a particular theme and following a planned order of worship. A hymn sing is an informal opportunity to sing hymns with leadership but using hymns chosen almost exclusively by the assembly. A hymn practice is a teaching and rehearsing session for learning ways to improve congregational singing and to master new hymns. Chapter 6 described how to plan and lead a hymn practice. This chapter discusses hymn festivals and hymn sings.

Recently I saw a sign in front of a museum inviting the public to visit its galleries and see its outstanding collection of art. The sign also stated that special exhibits were frequently displayed. I knew that in many museums their storage vaults contain many more works of art for which there is no room in their limited public galleries. The curators bring these up for special display from time to time and perhaps exchange some of them with pieces that have had their turn before the public.

It occurred to me that this was an analogy of the church and its hymns. If its hymnal contains 500-600 hymns, frequently only one tenth of this treasury are used in its stated services of worship. The rest are in the "basement storage vaults." Hymn festivals and hymn sings are opportunities to reach into this reserve, to learn and sing some of these treasures, and perhaps to add them to the repertory of familiar and loved hymns.

In the early 1930's Sir Walford Davies commented on the limited use which had been made of the treasures in one of the finest British hymnals, the *English Hymnal* 1906, edited by Ralph Vaughan Williams. He wrote: "Investigation would probably show that the choice of hymns in a normal parish church is surprisingly limited. There are, for example, many fine things in the *English Hymnal* that we, personally, have never, or very rarely, heard sung, during the thirty years of the book's existence. Now, as popular taste is more directly influenced by the songs and hymns that people sing communally, it is clear the the possibilities for good presented by contemporary hymn-books are not being developed."*

---

* *Music and Worship,* p. 194.

HYMN FESTIVALS

Hymn festivals are one of the means for exploring the hidden treasures of our hymnals. *The Stanza,* newsletter of The Hymn Society of America, carries lists of hymn festivals held across the country. These inspiring services, whether denominational or interdenominational, have been sponsored by groups such as rural or urban ministerial associations, an organists' guild chapter, a music club, a council of churches, The Hymn Society of America, or a local congregation.

Under expert leadership and surrounded by throngs of singers, a layperson usually gains a completely new experience of praise through song. This person takes back to the local congregation a new concept of stimulating, intelligent singing. The seeds of positive influence planted by such festivals are numberless.

The leader should be capable, well prepared, and vital. In a specific order for a hymn festival, it is probably wise to begin and end with a familiar hymns. In fact, in most circumstances, the majority of the hymns perhaps ought to be at least moderately familiar to most of the group. Vigorous hymns can be alternated with quieter ones for a change of mood. Every detail of the service should be meticulously planned. One hour's length seems to be the norm. Regardless of desired length, be sure to time every item so that the festival does not become over extended.

The singing can be varied by the use of descants, melody-in-the-tenor arrangements, varied harmonic accompaniments, and hymn concertatos. A variety of instrumental accompaniments adds interest. Alternation of stanzas between the various vocal forces (two sides of the congregation, men and women, congregation and choir, soloist and congregation) can be employed. Following the custom of good music radio commentators, use connective comments between hymns but make them brief, clear, and interesting. Omit certain stanzas upon occasion if desired and perhaps have the congregation read, not sing, some of the hymns or stanzas.

An excellent resource for planning, promoting, and directing a hymn festival is Austin C. Lovelace's *Hymn Festivals* which is Paper XXXI published by The Hymn Society of America, Texas Christian University, Fort Worth, TX 76129. Dr. Lovelace includes a history of the hymn festival movement, the purpose and function of a festival, types, planning procedures, resources and varied treatment of hymns. The paper concludes with some examples of festival orders.

He lists about 45 themes which have been used for festivals. Here are samples:

Lessons and Carols	Life of Christ
The Apostles' Creed	Hymns Based on the 23rd Psalm
Contemporary Hymns	Women Hymn Writers
Early American Folk Hymns	Hymns through the Ages
Welsh Hymns	God in Nature

In particular festivals it might be appropriate to include a dramatization of a hymn. Stories of hymns contain much material for drama. See, for example, Hal Hopson's *The Singing Bishop* which is a dramatized interpretation of the Palm Sunday hymn "All glory, laud, and honor." (See pages 11-12 for more information).

Festivals range from very simple format (a leader, piano/organ accompaniment, familiar hymns) to more elaborate singing occasions. I will give an example of the latter type so that you may see the variety of ways hymns can be used. Perhaps by studying this order you can decide which methods and materials you can adapt to your local situation.

A sample festival order

The following festival was a event in a large church music conference with over a thousand singers including organists/choir directors plus their choirs (children, youth, adult). Also available was a large bell choir, brass and wood-wind ensembles, organ and guitars.

As you study this order, note the following things:

Methods of using hymns. The congregation at one time or the other sang in unison, harmony and with or without accompaniment. On certain stanzas there were descants either sung or played on instruments (trumpet and flute). One hymn was treated as an extended anthem (concertato). There was considerable alternation of singing groups on stanzas.

Accompaniment. The congregation was accompanied at one time or the other by the organ, brass ensemble, flutes, and bell choirs.

Scope of hymns. Since the festival was designed to help musicians further explore their hymnals back home, note that we included a variety of types of texts and tunes: metrical and prose psalms, folk hymns, contemporary texts and tunes, and a responsorial psalm.

Mechanics. Because the hymnal did not contain some of the contemporary hymns, the complete scores of these were printed in the festival bulletin. Observe that sitting and standing instructions were clearly given in the margin.

SINGING PSALMS AND HYMNS

PRELUDES   Hymns and chorales played by brass ensemble and bell choir

PSALMS

METRICAL PSALMS

Stand   Psalm 100 "All people that on earth do dwell"   OLD HUNDREDTH

   Stanza 1. Unison   Ralph Vaughan Williams
     2. Unison — Adult/youth choirs harmony
     3. Adult choir with trumpet descant
     ⁕. Adult choir with melody in tenor
     5. Unison singing Doxology "Praise God from whom all blessings flow."
   Organ and brass

Sit   Psalm 139 "O Lord, my inmost heart and voice"   WALSALL

   Stanza 1. Unison
     2. Women unison
     3. Men unison
     4-5. Harmony

Sit   ### *SCOTTISH SCRIPTURE PARAPHRASE*
   Song of Simeon (*Nunc Dimittis*) Luke 2:23-33   DUNDEE
   (Text excerpt from *The Scottish Psalter 1929* was printed and sung unaccompanied)

Sit   ### *WATTS' PSALMS OF DAVID IMITATED*

   Psalm 146 "I'll praise my Maker while I've breath"
   Stanza 1. Unison
     2-3. Unison unaccompanied

Stand   Psalm 117 "From all that dwell below the skies"   LASST UNS ERFREUEN
   Stanza 1. Unison
     2. Unison antiphonal
     3. Unison/harmony

PSALM CHANT
Sit   Psalm 105 "Give thanks to the Lord"   Arranged by Paul Thomas

   Cantor and congregation

Al - le - lu - ia,   al - le - lu - ia, al - le - lu - ia.

Al - le - lu - ia,   al - le - lu - ia,   al - le - lu - ia.

Melchior Vulpius, c.1560-1616
Descant by Richard Proulx, © 1986, GIA Publications, Inc.

HYMNS

FOLK HYMN TUNES

Sit   **English** "All things bright and beautiful"   ROYAL OAK

Refrain before and after each stanza
Stanza 1. Women and girls
    2. Men and boys
    3. Women and girls
    4. Men and boys

Sit   **German** "Fairest Lord Jesus"   SCHÖNSTER HERR JESU
and ST. ELIZABETH

(The former tune sung on first and fourth stanzas and the latter on stanza two and three.)

Stand   **Irish** "O God, thou art the Father"   DURROW
Stanza 1. Unison
    2-3. Harmony

Sit   **Afro-American** "Go tell it on the mountain"   GO TELL IT ON
THE MOUNTAIN

Refrain in unison. Stanzas solo

Sit   **German** "On this day earth shall ring"   PERSONENT HODIE

Accompanied by handbells   Arranged by Gustav Holst

PENTATONIC TRADITIONAL TUNES

Sit   "Amazing grace, how sweet the sound"   NEW BRITAIN

Stand   "Come, you people, rise and sing"   BOUNDLESS MERCY

Sit   "How firm a foundation"   FOUNDATION

CONTEMPORARY HYMNS

Sit	"He is the Way"	NEW DANCE
	All stanzas unison. Accompanied by guitars.	
Sit	"Creating God, your fingers trace"	KEDRON
	Accompanied by organ and flute	
	(Hymn concertato arranged by Walter L. Pelz.	
	Published by Hope Publishing Company,	
	Carol Stream, IL 60188.	
	This hymn is quoted in Chapter 3.)	
Sit	"We are your people"	WHITFIELD
	(See Chapter 3)	
Stand	"Let all the world"	AUGUSTINE
	Unison and harmony (music by Erik Routley)	
Benediction "God be with you"		RANDOLPH

HYMN SINGS

Some of the most delightful hymn sings which I ever led were on summer Sunday evenings at a resort hotel on top of a mountain in New York State. Guests at this estate were invited to the enormous parlor with windows on three sides looking out over the lovely lake and the distant Catskills. Using an inter-denominational hymnal the guests and I sang numerous hymns, all of which were chosen by the guests except the final one which we called the Minne-waska hymn. It was Bishop Thomas Ken's "All praise to thee, my God, this night." We were able to sing a score or more hymns because we made an informal rule that we would sing only several stanzas of each hymn so that we could enjoy more choices.

Hymn sings are important partly because in many churches the people must always sing hymns chosen by someone else, usually the minister and/or the musician. Opportunities for these informal hymn singing occasions are numerous. I know of a congregation which sometimes devotes the entire program period at a church night supper to an all-request hymn sing. Another congregation invites members to come to the sanctuary fifteen minutes before the service, not for a hymn rehearsal, but to request and sing their own choice of hymns.

Various conferences offer opportunities for this method of hymn singing. A conference of church musicians included everything from hootenanny to traditional, evensongs utilizing guitars with an organ/synthesizer and jam sessions in hotel hallways.

A Conference on Aging devoted twenty minutes before the morning and evening assembly to an all-request hymn sing. As the people called for a favorite hymn, a concise bit of information about the text or tune was usually given.. When "All things bright and beautiful" was requested, I mentioned that the famous English veterinarian, James Herriot, named his four books after each of the lines of its refrain. And his obvious enjoyment of the beauties of the Yorkshire countryside was undoubtedly enhanced by his intimate knowledge of this hymn of nature.

It is significant to note that the hymns requested were not all the old tried and true favorites. These people frequently called for a hymn outside of the repertory of most congregations and this gave us a chance to introduce a hymn new to most of the people.

In Chapter 7 "Hymns in Homes," we mentioned several instances of family hymn sings and in Chapter 8 "Hymns and Education" we told about the Boyters and their family hymn sings using the childrens choirs as leaders.

RESOURCES/BIBLIOGRAPHY

ORGANIZATIONS
The Hymn Society of America
Texas Christian University, P. O. Box 30854, Fort Worth, TX 76129 (817) 921-7608.

Hymn Society Book Service. Its list of select titles of special interest includes books, hymnals and supplements, one-author collections of hymns, special hymn collections, and *Papers* of The Hymn Society.

The Hymn: A Journal of Congregational Song. Published quarterly.

The Stanza. A semi-annual newsletter.

The Society also sponsors workshops, hymn festivals, annual conferences, and offers advisory information. Free informational leaflet available.

American Guild of Organists. 475 Riverside Dr., Suite 1260, New York, NY 10015. (212) 870-2310.

Choristers Guild. 2834 W. Kingsley Rd., Garland, TX 75401. (214) 271-1521.

BIBLIOGRAPHY.
Clark, Keith C. *A Selective Bibliography for the Study of Hymns 1980.* Paper XXXIII of The Hymn Society of America.

COMPANION/HANDBOOKS
For a detailed listing of handbooks/guides/companions to hymnals, see Keith C. Clark's *A Bibliography of Handbooks and Companions to Hymnals: American, Canadian, and English.* This was published in four sections in *The Hymn* from July 1979 to April 1980. Following are a few selected titles of handbooks or collections of hymn stories:

Dearmer, Percy, compiler. *Songs of Praise Discussed.* London: Oxford University Press, 1933.

Gealy, Fred; Lovelace, A. C.; Young, Carlton R. *Companion to the Hymnal.* (Methodist, 1964, 1966). Nashville: Abingdon Press, 1970.

Hustad, Donald P. *Dictionary-Handbook to Hymns for the Living Church.* Carol Stream: Hope Publishing Company, 1978.

Osborne, Stanley L. *If Such Holy Song: The Story of The Hymn Book 1971.* Whitby, Ontario: The Institute of Church Music, 1976.

Reynolds, William J. *Companion to Baptist Hymnal.* [1975] Nashville: Broadman Press, 1976.

Routley, Erik. *An English-Speaking Hymnal Guide.* Chicago: G.I.A. Publications, 1979.

Ronander, Albert C.; Porter, Ethel K. *Guide to the Pilgrim Hymnal.* Philadelphia: United Church Press, 1966.

Stulken, Marilyn Kay, *Hymnal Companion to the Lutheran Book of Worship.* Philadelphia: Fortress Press, 1981.

DEVELOPMENT OF CONGREGATIONAL SINGING

Eskew, Harry; McElrath, Hugh T. *Sing with Understanding: An Introduction to Christian Hymnology.* Nashville: Broadman Press, 1980.

Ferguson, John Allen. *A Mini-Course in Creative Hymn Playing.* New York: American Guild of Organists.

Kemp, Helen. *Music in Church Education with Children.* Garland, TX: Choristers Guild, 1970.

Lovelace, Austin; Rice, William. *Music and Worship in the Church.* Revised and Enlarged Edition. Nashville: Abingdon Press, 1976.

Lovelace, Austin. *The Anatomy of Hymnody.* Chicago: G.I.A. Publications, Inc., 1982.

_____ *The Organist and Hymn Playing.* Revised. Carol Stream: Agape, 1981.

_____ *Hymn Notes for Church Bulletins.* Chicago: G.I.A. Publications, Inc., 1987.

Mealy, Margaret. *34 Easy Hymn Accompaniments for Organ.* Chicago: G.I.A. Publications, Inc.

Ogasapian, John. *Church Organs: A Guide to Selection and Purchase.* New York: American Guild of Organists.

Reynolds, William J. *Congregational Singing.* Nashville: Convention Press, 1975.

Riedel, Scott R. *Acoustics in the Worship Space.* Church Music Pamphlet Series, Carl Schalk, editor. St. Louis: Concordia Publishing House, 1986.

Sydnor, James Rawlings. *Hymns and Congregational Singing.* Atlanta: John Knox Press, 1960.

_____ *Hymns & Their Uses.* Carol Stream: Agape, 1982.

_____ *Hymns: a Congregational Study.* Carol Stream: Agape, 1983

HISTORY AND PRACTICE OF HYMNODY

Benson, Louis F. *The English Hymn: Its Development and Use in Worship.* 1915. Reprint 1962 by John Knox Press.

_____ *The Hymnody of the Christian Church.* Philadelphia: Westminster Press, 1927. Reprint, 1956, John Knox Press.

Davies, Walford; Harvey Grace. *Music & Worship.* New York: The H. W. Gray Company, 1935. Reprinted by AMS Press, New York, NY.

Parker, Alice. *Creative Hymn Singing.* Chapel Hill: Hinshaw Music Inc.

Patrick, Millar. *The Story of the Church's Song.* 1927. Second edition revised 1962. John Knox Press.

Reynolds, William J. *A Survey of Christian Hymnody.* Carol Stream: Agape, 1987.

Routley, Erik. *A Panorama of Christian Hymnody.* Chicago: G.I.A. Publications, 1979.

_____ *Christian Hymns Observed.* Prestige Publishers, 1982.

_____ *Church Music and the Christian Faith.* Carol Stream: Agape, 1978.

_____ *The Music of Christian Hymns.* Chicago: G.I.A. Publications, 1981.

Schilling, S. Paul. *The Faith We Sing,* Philadelphia: Westminster Press, 1983.

CONCORDANCES, DICTIONARIES, INDEXES, HYMNBOOK COLLECTIONS

Diehl, Katharine Smith. *Hymns and Tunes-an Index.* Metuchen, NJ: Scarecrow Press, 1966

Hunnicutt, Judy. *Index of Biblical Characters in Hymns.* The Hymn Society of America.

_____ *Index of Hymn Tune Accompaniments for Organ.* The Hymn Society of America.

Julian, John, editor. *A Dictionary of Hymnology.* Reprint 1977 by Gordon Press.

McDormand, Thomas B.; Crossman, Frederic S. *Judson Concordance to Hymns.* Valley Forge: The Judson Press, 1965.

Porter, Ellen Jane L. *Hymnbook Collections of North America.* Published by The Hymn Society of America.

Sadie, Stanley, editor. *The New Grove Dictionary of Music and Musicians.* 20 vol. London: Macmillan Publishers, Ltd. 1980.

Schalk, Carl, editor. *Key Words in Church Music.* St. Louis: Concordia Publishing House, 1978.

INDEX